LOVE'S
Golden
Wings

Other Books by LaJoyce Martin:

The Harris Family Saga:
To Love a Bent-Winged Angel
Love's Mended Wings
Love's Golden Wings
When Love Filled the Gap
To Love a Runaway
A Single Worry
Two Scars Against One
The Fiddler's Song
The Artist's Quest

Pioneer Romance:
The Wooden Heart
Heart-Shaped Pieces
Light in the Evening Time
To Strike a Match
Love's Velvet Chains
Destiny's Winding Road

Historical Romance:
So Swift the Storm
So Long the Night

Historical Novel:
Thread's End

Western:
The Other Side of Jordan
To Even the Score

Path of Promise:
The Broken Bow
Ordered Steps

Children's Short Stories:
Batteries for My Flashlight

Nonfiction:
Mother Eve's Garden Club
Heroes, Sheroes, and a Few Zeroes
I'm Coming Apart, Lord!
Alpha-Toons

Order from:
Pentecostal Publishing House
8855 Dunn Road
Hazelwood, MO 63042-2299

LOVE'S

LaJoyce
Martin

Golden
Wings

Love's Golden Wings

by LaJoyce Martin

©1987 Word Aflame Press
Hazelwood, MO 63042-2299
Printing History: 1990, 1992, 1995, 1998

Cover Design by Tim Agnew
Illustrated by Art Kirchoff

All Scripture quotations in this book are from the King James Version of the Bible unless otherwise identified.

Printed in United States of America.

WORD AFLAME®PRESS
8855 DUNN ROAD
HAZELWOOD, MO 63042-2299

Library of Congress Cataloging-in-Publication Data

Martin, LaJoyce, 1937-
    Love's golden wings.

    (LaJoyce Martin's Pioneer trilogy ; bk. 3)
    I. Title.   II. Series: Martin, LaJoyce, 1937-
Pioneer trilogy ; bk. 3.
PS3563.A72486L55   1987   813'.54   87-17346
ISBN 0-932581-19-6

To
my family and friends
and
to the memory of
Dream

Contents

Preface

In 1984 a special horse came into our lives. She was a beautiful chestnut mare with a white blaze face, but perhaps the magic of memory has made her even more beautiful than what she really was. Who knows?

After bringing our fifteen-year-old daughter, Angela, a few days of happiness, the special horse quietly exited our lives, leaving us sadder but richer of heart.

The following account of Dream was written by my husband, Elroy Martin, not for publication or the critique of professionals, but from his heart. I have not tried to reconstruct or embellish his story. To do so would be to lose its poignancy.

*   *   *

She was a Dream.

She came suddenly into our lives, borne by a tragedy.

We found her in tall, dry, dead weeds and grass between a four-lane expressway and a dry, empty stream bed, in a wallow made by her restless turning on wounded, sore limbs. She was really too injured to move, but we could not leave her where she would not receive proper, tender, loving care.

Struggling to her feet, she bravely responded to the call, "Come on, baby. I know it hurts, but you must come on, baby!" And come she did—through deep, dry grass and weeds that roughly raked every wound she had received by sliding down the clawing concrete embankment on her knees and side; through knee-deep mud; then into a waiting trailer; and finally to a barn, a stall, and journey's end.

For several weeks we took special care of her, fighting to save her mangled joints. She was sometimes better, sometimes worse, but mostly worse. But she was a Dream.

She had a fine head, bright eyes, and a quick mind. Why even her registry knew she was special, for she proudly wore the name "Triple's Dream." She caressed us with her nose as we, the girl and I, dressed and swabbed her wounds, but to no avail.

With eyes still alert, ears perked, head high, she met the vet who came to put her to sleep. Like a giant tree, she tumbled and was still. Over? No, it was not over. She was a Dream.

When school was out, the girl asked, first thing, "How's my Dream?"

Her daddy had to break the news, "We put her to sleep today."

"But, Daddy, I wanted to see her before she died."

"I'm sorry."

"Have they come and got her yet?"

"No. Do you want to see her?"

"Yes!" Quickly she changed into boots and jacket to protect herself against the cold, damp weather. After a quiet ride to the field, she said, "Daddy, I want to go by myself."

"Okay, honey."

Straight to her Dream she went and then knelt to caress her neck and ears. With fingers nimble and tender, she entwined her memories into the mane of her Dream. As the wind swept the girl's long hair to one side, she told her Dream goodbye.

Resolutely she rose to turn and walk away, leaving her Dream. Once, only once, she paused to look back, drawn by some sudden call of her heart. Looking back for the last time, she advanced into the days ahead, with her Dream only in her mind.

After the remains of Dream were carried away, the aged black man, Moses Hill, called to give us the address where we were to send payment for the expenses of her removal. "Ma'am, I picked up his horse for him. But Ma'am, there was a little red ribbon tied in its mane, and a small gold pin. Ma'am, I sorta figgered it was a child what done it."

The horse was never ridden by the young girl, only loved and nursed through pain-filled, hopeless days.

Is Dream dead? No! For the girl now rides through perfect days of the mind, in verdant fields, and peaceful valleys, in places she could never have gone, in ways that could not have been—always on her Dream.

Whether in crowds amid pressure or alone in the solitude of her room, when she needs to, she saddles up, climbs up and rides away on a Dream.

* * *

Love's Golden Wings, the third book in a series, begins with the birth of a very special horse.

Chapter 1

The White Mustang

"Amy, come and see what the Lord has placed in our care!" Joseph stood at the back door wiping his hands, still soiled from the birth, on his denim trousers.

Most ranchers would have shot the crippled filly. But Joseph wasn't most ranchers.

Amy watched as the brood mare, devoid of human prejudices and oblivious to imperfections nuzzled her baby lovingly. "What's her problem, Joseph?"

"Bowed tendons."

"Will she ever. . .walk?"

"Only with difficulty. She'll never be. . .useful. Except as a pet. Won't Effie love her?"

"Won't she!"

"She'll be something Effie can call her own when she comes to visit."

"And identify with. What'll we name her?"

Joseph grinned. "If she's mischievous, I'll call her the bent-winged devil."

"And if she's good?"

"We'll leave that up to Effie."

"Shall I write her about the colt?" Amy bent to croon a gentle encouragement to the newborn foal and looked into its curious, intelligent eyes. The small animal sniffed at Amy's hand with her moist nose. "She's a heart-stealer, Joseph."

"Just tell Effie we have a surprise for her, Amy."

No more than ten minutes back inside brought to Amy's ears the faint sounds of a wagon approaching. She laid aside her mending and hastened to the front door. Visitors in this isolated region of the territory were rare.

Shading her eyes, she saw that it was Dave Browning's rig. It was apparent that no emergency brought the driver on this mission, judging by the leisurely speed and the old horse chosen for the mount.

The road that stretched to meet the conveyance was little more than two narrow tracks, beaten out by the coming and going of wooden wheels. Sandwiched between the grooves were infrequent clumps of bear grass that tantalized the horses.

Grace Browning threw up a friendly hand as Amy walked to the gate to meet her. The sun emphasized the seams sewn on her face by years of cheerful smiles.

"Cousin Grace! Come sit a spell!" welcomed Amy eagerly.

"I found the day simply begging an outing! Have you ever seen a lovelier spring? And I'm bursting with good news!" Grace removed her slat bonnet and smoothed her chestnut hair.

Amy led the way into the newly constructed house, its cracker-box shape divided into four large segments and a pantry. Her pampered grandmother, accustomed to an eighteen-room estate in the populated East, would have scorned the crudeness of the cottage, but Amy loved it. Her husband's hands had fashioned it, stowing little pieces of his heart here and there among the boards.

"I know you're glad to get settled into your new home," Grace Browning acknowledged, "but I miss you dreadfully from the stage stop! Your room at the inn echoes empty."

"I think you put up with us quite long enough," laughed Amy. "Joseph misses your salt-rising bread though. I haven't perfected that recipe yet."

"I brought you a letter that came by post last evening." Grace handed the mail to Amy, who put it on the mahogany desk to open after her guest departed.

"Will you have some tea, Grace?"

"I wouldn't mind if I did, thank you, Amy. I took my time getting here." She glanced at the grandfather clock that nearly touched the ceiling. "Just a bit over an hour on the road. It's like rolling back the calendar twenty years to come to this place."

"Has it been that long since Aunt Rebecca and Uncle Charles staked claim on this land?"

"Lacking one year. They came out right after they were married in 1872. Effie was born in 1875, and Charles left here when Rebecca died in '78. I'm pretty good on dates."

"I should say you are!"

"I'll never forget the afternoon they rolled into the Caprock Coachhouse. It was late October, and they'd been

15

on the trail for three months. The nights were getting frosty around the edges. Rebecca looked so young and sweet and. . .trusting, that's the word. Her adoration for Charles showed in her lovely violet eyes. My Charlotte was about six years old, just beginning her letters. She was Rebecca's devoted slave from the start.

"Charles carried a tattered map given to him by Jim's father, James Collins, a stage driver who worked the route from Independence, Missouri, to Santa Fe. He knew this part of the country well, and directed Charles to this piece of property. James Collins was an old friend of Charles's father.

"So anxious were the young couple to occupy their land that they lived in a sort of makeshift dugout for a few weeks until Charles could throw up a one-room cabin. Rebecca didn't bring much with her in the way of worldly possessions, though it was evident she came from a high class family. As I remember, she had some quilts and dishes her mother had insisted on her bringing. She had a real pretty doll she brought along for her first daughter, her Bible, and some simple clothing. That was about it.

"Dave helped Charles all he could, but Charles was fiercely independent. They had bad luck right from the start. A horse and a cow died the first winter. But Charles had more than his share of 'grit and gumption' as they say. Reverses delayed the building of a new home for Rebecca, but never erased Charles's optimism for ultimate success. 'We have the rest of our lives on our land,' he would say. 'Eventually the tide will turn.'

"But it didn't. No, it didn't." Grace shook her head. "The second winter, Rebecca got word that both of her parents had died of malaria. Charles offered to return with her to her home country, but she would hear none of it. You know what she said? She said, 'This is my home. I'd rather die here than return there.'"

"I. . .admire Rebecca," Amy interspersed.

"You and Rebecca were cut out of the same yard of goods."

"Then Effie was born?"

"Yes, about midway through the time of occupancy necessary to secure a homestead claim. And nothing short of Rebecca's determination could have coaxed her through her first listless weeks of life. The inn was rip-roaring with business back then, and I had little leisure time to help the new mother. Charles came in for a tonic now and then, saying the baby wasn't well. He worked long hours to keep the wolf of hunger from attacking his family.

"I thought Effie just got off to a slow start, but looking back now, I think Rebecca knew that the child would always be. . .special. She channeled all her reserves of energy into the mainstream of teaching Effie the babyhood basics, forgetting herself, neglecting her own physical and mental nourishment. She was too weak to fight off the fever when it came.

"Charles found her dead. She was slumped on the braided rug near the sleeping child, a spoon still in her hand. She had expended the last ounce of her ebbing strength trying to care for Effie.

"Charles didn't even come and get us to share his grief. He buried her. . .alone, then left the next day to take Effie to Joseph's folks in Texas. The wilderness land had lost its gilt-edged beauty for him. . .Rebecca was his life."

"It's a pity they couldn't have been buried together."

17

"Charles and Rebecca will always be together, no matter where they're buried."

"It seems. . .ironic. . .enjoying the beautiful land they struggled so hard for. What's the old saying—we suffer without succeeding so that others may succeed without suffering?"

"Your Aunt Rebecca cherished every minute of the suffering, if that makes any sense. She lived more in her short span on earth than most people live in their threescore and ten."

"Effie said she liked sunsets and rainbows and butterflies."

"That was Rebecca."

"Was Charles like Joseph?"

"As much like Joseph as you are like Rebecca. Having you two on the land is like having Charles and Rebecca back."

"I feel almost. . .guilty having things so comfortable. Why this house is heaven compared to the cabin with the dirt floor that she lived in!"

"Charles planned grandly for her and the baby. He shared his dreams with Dave and me. A person can bear much deprivation if he has dreams."

"But it seems. . .sinful to have such conveniences as these," Amy swept the room with a gesture of her hand. "Jonathan insisted that I have our mother's furniture. He's a brother with an enlarged heart when it comes to sharing."

"Brothers like Jonathan don't come in bunches. They don't even come one to a family. You're fortunate. Oh, and by the way, he isn't married yet, I don't suppose?"

Amy sighed. "I hope not. The young lady he has eyes

for is. . .not his type. She isn't a Christian. She knows
Jonathan inherited some money from Grandfather. I'm
trying to get Jonathan to come out and help Joseph for
a while. If I could get him out of her grasp, he'd see things
differently."

"Is Joseph building fences today?"

"No, he's horse-doctoring. One of the mares just had
a colt. Our very first. She's solid white."

"How exciting! A *white* mustang?"

"Joseph says they are somewhat rare."

"It must be a little beauty."

"It's. . .a cripple."

"You won't keep it then?"

"Oh, yes. Joseph couldn't destroy anything. He's too
tenderhearted. After seeing the little thing, I think he'd
have to shoot me first! It stole my heart."

"Those kind are easy to get attached to."

"We have Effie in mind. Since she's a cripple too,
they'll get on royally."

"Now won't they! Seems God knows just where to
send His bent-winged angels to provide them with plenty of tender love and care."

Amy refilled Grace's cup, setting out spiced tea cakes
for each of them. "But you said *you* had good news."

"That I do! Charlotte and Jim are the proud parents
of a big boy born a week ago the Saturday past. They
named him Joseph James. Jim calls him J. J."

"Your first grandchild! I can't believe you're not on
your way to Santa Fe this minute."

"Oh, I probably would be, but Jim and Charlotte are
bringing the baby here as soon as mother and son are able
to travel. They want you and Joseph to see Joseph's

19

namesake."

"Why, that's reason for a celebration, Grace!"

The animated chatter continued until Grace's eyes again ventured to the hands of the grandfather clock, finding the hour hand dropping perceptibly. The whir and gong would soon announce four o'clock. She jumped up hurriedly, retrieving her bonnet. "But I must go posthaste," she announced. "Dave will be wanting his supper. And if guests happen to be at the inn, he'll be in a frenzy."

"But come again. . .and often," Amy insisted, escorting her to the gate. Grace, a veteran of the territory for more than a quarter of a century, was unaffected by the dropping temperature that announced eve's approach, but Amy shivered. Winter's lease was up, and although the season moved out on schedule, it left the door ajar, letting in the cold air as night advanced.

Amy watched her cousin twice removed merge into the horizon, leaving behind an empty trail flanked by an occasional yucca plant that displayed a large panicle of white blossoms, standing head high like a lone sentinel, regal and posture-perfect. The yucca was Amy's favorite arborescent plant. It shot up through fibrous-margined leaves from a woody base. She fondly called it the lily of the wilderness.

The place where she stood united two diverse topographies: the desert with its shimmery-covered sand dunes in front of her, and their own land, a verdant cul-de-sac tucked in a horseshoe-shaped oasis outlined by an arroyo, behind her.

James Collins had given Charles Harris a map that navigated him to this wonderful nook of nature. And by some quirk of fate it was destined to be Harris land forever. Effie was born here. Rebecca died here. Now she and Joseph planted their hearts in this soil. And today their first colt was born, severely handicapped.

No, it isn't fate, she thought. *It's the will of God.*

Amy sat down on the horsehair sofa to read the letter Grace Browning had brought.

Chapter 2

Party Minus the
Ice Cream

"*I* got th' ice, Martha." Henry unwrapped the crystal clear blocks that had necessitated a special trip to the ice house in The Springs and placed them into the top compartment of the wooden icebox.

"I'll thank you an' th' boys to turn th' crank on th' ice cream freezer fer me, Henry," she replied. "You didn't ferget th' salt, did ya?"

"No, I didn't ferget. You gonna make peach ice cream er plain?"

"Plain. An' then anybody can put peaches on theirn what wants to."

Effie's birthday dawned cloudless and warm, awash with Central Texas's own decorative bluebonnets. Martha planned the birthday party, decking the ample parlor with vases of the abundant wild flowers.

Six months ago the carpenters from town had loaded their tools and ridden away, leaving behind a simple, seven-room, white clapboard farmhouse with two rock chimneys and a wraparound porch.

Effie, the benefactor, had suggested a grand structure with an upper chamber and balcony, but Martha, her pride of yesteryear conquered, protested.

"All we need is somethin' simple an' comfortable," she insisted. "We live in a modest neighborhood among hard-workin' farmers. 'Tain't fittin' that we should live high an' mighty like kings while those'ns 'round 'bout us live plain. Anyways we don't want to take advantage o' Effie's kindness. She needs to save 'er money fer th' future."

"Besides," she told Effie, "me an' you couldn't climb stairs too good." Martha's left side, impaired by a stroke two years before, was still weak, and she walked with a limp.

To Henry she had given her chief instructions about the house. "Jest so they build th' parlor plenty big enough fer our fam'ly reunions, parties, an' weddin's. Cause we'll have lots in th' years to come." Standing in this picturesque parlor now, she took a last look at the pleasing flower arrangements and nodded her head, satisfied with what she saw. The room was right for the first party.

After supper, the guests started arriving, bringing gifts and cheer. Sarah brought the cake embellished with sixteen candles. "Happy birthday, sister!" She kissed Effie.

Parson Stevens, his good wife and his daughter, Pauline, came, followed by the Gibsons. The oldest Gibson girl, Eunice, brought her new husband. Miss Vivian hobbled along on her cane, greeted by all her former students. Wizened little old Mr. Rogers trailed along with his rotund wife, and Sister Myrt, the outdated church organist, showed up with her usual self-righteous airs, fretting about the dangers of worldly possessions and falling from grace.

In the back yard, Henry cranked the new freezer while Chester sat atop a gunnysack to stabilize the contraption, rising now and then to let Henry add salt and ice. When a steady trickle of salty water ran from the small hole near the top of the wooden bucket into the tub below, Henry strained to put more pressure on the handle. "It's afreezin' all right!" he grinned proudly, giving the impression that he had not been sure the process would work.

Martha put her head out the back door. "Set th' freezer on th' back stoop to keep till we're ready fer it," she said.

Those who had not seen the house were conducted on a tour of the place. Much of the lovely old furniture had belonged to Effie's grandmother, Margaret Franklin. Cousin Jonathan had shipped it to The Springs by rail. A Boston rocker sat near Effie's bed; her heating stove boasted a newfangled isinglass front.

The resplendent kitchen gleamed with a late model cookstove, complete with a warming shelf, and a modern icebox. The dining table shone with new checkered oilcloth while harvest benches replaced the sagging cane-bottom chairs of the old house. The children, who had never seen such grandeur, whispered to each other.

But the most imposing room of all was the elegant carpeted and wallpapered parlor. The grand settee from the Franklin estate made Sister Myrt gasp and mumble about the pride of life. Gargoyle wall sconces, such as Effie had seen in Charlotte and Jim's adobe home in Santa Fe, held brass lamps. Sister Myrt probably considered these outright idolatrous. Effie had found in the Sears and Roebuck order book decor similar to Charlotte's and had had Dessie fill out the order sheet, disregarding price and surprising Martha.

No homestead in Brazos Point had ever hosted such a party. Children laughed and played, friends chatted, and oldtimers exchanged stories, the buzz of excitement reminding Effie of a beehive. Outside, fireflies glowed in the gathering dusk, winking sporadically.

"Blow out yer candles an' make a wish, Effie! Quick!" Alan urged. *What more could anyone wish for than family, friends, and plenty?* she wondered. In a sweeping breath, Effie extinguished the tiny flames, cheered by a clapping applause. She closed her eyes tightly. *I'll wish to go see Joseph and Amy,* she told herself.

"Now don't tell nobody what you wished," instructed Alan, "an' it'll shore come true."

"Are you ready fer me to bring in th' freezer, Martha?" Henry asked. Martha nodded, putting a ladle into the great crock bowl of sweetened peaches.

Henry stepped out the back door and was gone so long that Martha went to learn the reason. He wandered about, bewildered. "What's th' matter, Henry?" His strange actions concerned her.

"I can't find th' ice cream, Martha."

"Are you havin' a memory lapse? Ain't it right where you left it?"

"No, it ain't. Som'body's done gone an' moved it an' I can't find it nowheres."

"It's a prank th' boys er playin' on you, Henry," Martha chided. "They knowed where you set it to keep."

"No, Martha. 'Tain't th' boys' doin's. I asked 'em. They hain't even been back here nohow."

"Well Henry, it couldn't'a jest disappeared into thin air."

"I guess it could'uv. That's what it seems to have done."

Further searching produced no ice cream freezer. The party proceeded minus the anticipated highlight of the night—a first batch of vanilla ice cream made in the new freezer.

"Could a dog'a drug it off, Henry?" puzzled Martha.

"No possible way, Martha."

"You don't reckon somebody got it?"

"I don't know who. Ever'body's accounted fer 'cept Matthew, an' he's in college."

"An' if'n Matthew *did* come, he'd be more interested in Pauline Stevens than in ice cream!"

While the Harris party reveled into the night with music and laughter, two characters of ill repute squatted on the earthen floor of the old Robbins barn less than a half mile away, enjoying vanilla ice cream by the light of a pine knot.

"Yep. I lived in this here dump fer four, maybe five months onct," Claude Grimes told his cohort, a seedy youth that he referred to as Spurs. "Had to git out in a hurry, though. Paw got into trouble an' got th' law on our trail. We left like blue blazes."

Spurs laughed coarsely. "Has they ever been a time you *hadn't* had th' law on yer trail, Claude?"

"I ain't behind bars yet, am I? Ain't been hanged yet,

have I? Ner even horsewhupped. An' I ain't plannin' on gettin' caught this time neither."

"How'd you learn about this girl. . .what's her name. . . ?"

"Effie."

". . .havin' money?"

"I got aholt of a letter th' school teacher, Miss Amy, wrote my sister Sonny, tellin' as how they found th' relative they was lookin' fer when we was here in school—an' that kin happened to be a simpleton girl named Effie. I knew they was lookin' fer th' relative to settle up a big estate."

"Maybe 'twas jest a rumor."

"Ha!" spat Claude. "Did ya see that new spread what's been built? They fell into some money all right. An' it wasn't jest pennies an' nickels, neither. Why, when I lived here they was poor as Job's turkey an' lived in a *shack.*"

"But what exactly decided you to plan this. . . ?"

"I got tired'a beatin' my brains out fer six bits a day. Now take Paw fer instance. He never worked a day in 'is life an' made powerful good money makin' bootleg whiskey. Made more money in a month than. . ."

"If'n yore Paw made sech powerful good money, why was you'ns livin' in this here dump?"

Claude's cold brown eyes shot daggers in the light of the pine knot. "Spurs, yore crowdin' me, boy. One thing you don't *never* do is question my Paw's integrity."

"Sorry, Claude. Honest."

A moment of sinister silence reigned, and Spurs sat stone still as if fearing to breathe, petrified by Claude's raging countenance. Then the storm passed and Claude was again in control.

"As I was sayin' 'fore I got rudely interrupted, I got tired'a slavin' on a reg'lar job fer peanuts. Why, it'd take way more'n a year to make five hundred flat at th' wages I was makin'."

"Now yore gonna divvy up with me, ain't you?"

"This is my idee an' you ain't deservin' o' half. . ."

"Then I won't write th' note."

"Okay. Okay. You drive a hard bargain, Spurs, but it'll be share an' share alike. You'll have to write th' note 'cause if'n th' same teacher's still here, she'll recognize my handwritin'. An' since you never been here, nobody'll recognize your'n."

"So we'll ask fer a thousand dollars ransom fer th' kid?"

"We'll be obliged to ask that much since you charge sech exorbant prices to write a measly little ole note."

"An' what if'n th' family don't feel like th' retarded kid is worth a thousand dollars to 'um?"

"Spurs, you ain't been 'round here. That's evident. 'Cause if'n you had'uv, you'd know that that kid is th' pick o' th' community—th' family's pet, th' preacher's pet, th' teacher's pet, an' all. They'll give any amount to get 'er back! Trust me, 'cause I know. But we wouldn't want to overdo it an' ask fer more'n they can come up with."

"Why's she so important?"

"Beats me. Seems I heared she saved her baby sister from a fire er somethin' like that. An' they all feel indebted to 'er."

"How we gonna git 'er?"

"Won't be hard. A cake job. They don't even have a watchdog to bark. An' th' kid faints when she gits scared. I put a lizard in her lunchbox one day at school an' she went out like a light."

"Honest you did?" Spurs slapped his knee in mocking laughter.

"Yep. Teacher threatened to expel me fer it, but I up an' quit school. Beat 'er to th' punch. Anyways, as I was sayin', when th' girl sees us an' learns our intentions, she'll pass out neat-like. She's not big as a minute, an' she's a cripple besides. Can't fight back."

"But how'll we *find* 'er?"

"I done studied all that out, Spurs. She has her own room. We'll just crawl in 'er winder an' threaten to kill her if'n she makes a sound. Paw shot 'er brother onct, so she'll believe me."

"You're sure this is gonna work, Claude?"

"Got no doubts. My plan is foolproof."

"This shore is good ice cream. Reckon they've missed it at th' big party yet?"

"I dunno, but it'd been better if'n you'd'a slipped in th' kitchen an' got them there peaches."

"I may look dumb, Claude, but I ain't *that* dumb."

Claude guffawed. "Spurs, you're jest a yeller coward, that's what. But yore fixin' up to be a *rich* yeller coward, mind you."

Chapter 3

First Letter

*J*oseph stopped in his tracks when he saw Amy sitting on the sofa reading the letter, her violet eyes misty with emotion.

"Is it. . .bad news, love?"

She shook her head, regaining her voice. "No, it's so. . .sweet. Your mother wrote this letter herself."

"My *mother* wrote the letter? But Amy, that's impossible."

"It's Mom Harris's own handwriting. And Joseph, it's. . .beautiful!"

"But. . .except for signing her name, Mother never learned to write. She. . .never had a chance to get an education."

"Until now. Effie has taken it upon herself to teach Mom to read and write. I'm so proud of Mom! And brave, patient Effie! What would any of us have done without

Effie?''

She handed the letter to Joseph, who stared at it in disbelief.

"Read it," she said, "and see for yourself."

My dear childern (it read)

This is my furst lettr. Effie is techin me my lettrs n words. I have time now that awl the childern is frum underfeet. Effie is a gud techer n proud of me. We started one year past n she says Im lerning so fast.

Yur sistr Sarah n Hanks babe boy is growin big. Michael (I ask Effie how to spel that) is one years nest month. He is helthy n a joy to his gran-pap. Me to.

Matthew n Palline is planin to get marry in June when he is threw collage. They wont you to come fer the weddin. We wont to no can you come. Question.

We have a new hous fixt n we have plenty rooms. I had the pawlor bilt big fer famly gathrins. Its perdy.

Parson Stevns mother died. She was past her thre skore n 10 beside in ill helth a long time.

Paw n the youngens send greetns. Effie especial.

May God bless n kep you n caus His face to shine upawn you.

Love,
Mother

"Effie's worth her weight in pure gold." Joseph gave the letter back to Amy, shaking his head in admiration, wiping happy tears from his eyes.

Amy reached for his hand to share the tender moment. "She's built them a new home with part of her money. She told me that was her plan. I picture it as a massive estate with many gables and an elegant winding staircase with burnished banisters that tempt Chester, Arthur, and Alan to slide down them. What is your idea of it?"

"I have it pictured rather simple, possibly without an upstairs at all. At one time, Mother would have insisted on an elaborate homestead, showy and pretentious, but she has changed so much in these last few years. When Uncle Charles left Effie and went to California for gold, promising Mother a fortune when he returned, she went into a tizzy of planning for a mansion that would have rivaled the White House for beauty. She wanted dishes . . .clothes. . .furniture better and more expensive than any of her neighbors. Pride lay at the root of it all. But now. . .since Effie saved Sally's life and Mother had the stroke. . .*things* don't matter like they used to. Now she wouldn't *want* anything so much nicer than the other folk in the community."

"Joseph?"

"Yes, dear?"

"Was Effie always so. . .*good?*"

Joseph wrinkled his brow in thought before answering. "Effie was never a *bad* child, but something happened when she was about nine or ten years old that changed her life. I remember it well. Effie and I were always close in heart."

"Tell me about it." Amy still held his hand, giving it a loving squeeze.

"She had had an especially bad day. Mother was on her case, cross and resentful. Mother actually almost hated Effie. She was ashamed of her and hid her away from society because she was a cripple. Back then, a lot of people from the old school felt that a physical defect was caused by evil spirits, demon possession. Effie tried everything in her power to earn Mother's love, but nothing worked. As I remember, she tried to take Mother a cup of hot coffee to appease her, but tripped and spilled it, splashing some on Mother's foot. Mother yelled at her unmercifully. Effie took her wounded heart to the woodshed, where she spent a good deal of her time. I had heard her there crying—and I figured she was praying—on numerous occasions. On this particular day, she didn't come in for supper. Just before sundown, Dessie went to check on her and found her in a trance of some sort. When Dessie awoke her, she talked perfect English without stuttering for the first time, telling Dessie what had happened to her."

"What had happened?"

"She said she had a vision of the Lord. And I don't doubt it. She had been reading the Bible for days. But what amazed me was that her face seemed to. . .glow. And she was happy even though she had no reason to be. From that day on, she showed love even when she was mistreated; she was kind regardless."

"Did you ever talk to her about this. . .experience?"

"Yes, I did. She said she didn't have words to explain it—that she spoke to Jesus in a new language and that she had never felt such. . .joy."

34

"And she was different after that?"

"She was. There was a. . .peace about her. Dessie wanted the same kind of peace, but Mother caught them in the woodshed praying and forbade Dessie ever to go to the shed with Effie again after that. She thought Effie was demented, possessed, talking to spirits."

"But you knew her new-found peace was a gift from God?"

"I had no doubts."

"I'd like to talk to Effie about it sometime."

"She loves to talk about it, but for years Mother wouldn't let her even mention it."

"Will we be able to go back for Matthew's wedding next June? That's not so very far away."

"I would like to. Would you mind making the long trip?"

"I'd love it! Matthew would be disappointed if you weren't there, and Pauline would be disappointed if I wasn't. Besides, I want to see which of us has the right mental picture of that new house!"

"The rail connections are good from Amarillo to The Springs. We can make it in two days barring a locomotive breakdown or a washed out bridge. And that's always a possibility."

"Aren't trains wonderful?"

"I never dreamed I'd admit it. I balk at modernization. But they are mighty. . .convenient."

"Don't tell me you resented the trains for putting an end to your stagecoach driving?" Amy's dark eyes twinkled.

"Not after I met you." Joseph grinned. "My coach driving would have ended anyway."

"Oh, Joseph, you're sweet."

"Not always."

"Now what do you mean by that?"

"I think I need some of whatever Effie has to be better *inside*. As hard as I try to be upright, sometimes I don't feel very successful."

"Sometimes I feel the same way, Joseph."

Amy traced a love message on his hand with the tip of her finger. "Joseph?"

"Yes, Amy?"

"Do you suppose they would let us bring Effie home with us to stay until next spring?"

"It would take some tall talking. You know how Mother is about Effie. Especially since her stroke."

"I could help Effie finish up her schooling. She's so far ahead, she doesn't lack much, I'm sure."

"I know Effie would want to come, but she wouldn't come against Mother's wishes."

"Why don't we make it a matter of prayer, Joseph?"

"Let's do that."

"By the way, how's the new colt?"

"Struggling for survival, but you never saw such a will to live!"

"I was going to write Effie about our surprise."

"Maybe you'd better wait a few more days and make sure."

"But Joseph, it. . .the pony *has* to live."

Joseph kissed Amy's hand. "Do you know, little wife, that we are probably the only two people on earth that would *want* a crippled foal to live?"

"Really?"

"Most people would consider the firstling of our herd

a bad omen."

"Oh, but she's a good omen!" protested Amy. "Just consider our Effie. What if she hadn't been born? What if she hadn't lived? Sally would have died in the fire! You and I would never have married! Mom and Dad Harris would not have a new house! We wouldn't have our land here! Why, Effie is the best thing that ever happened!"

Joseph laughed. "Slow down long enough to get your breath. I'll do my best to see that the filly lives. But. . .I'm sure God has something to say about all this."

Chapter 4

Kidnapped!

"*C*an we go afishin'? Please, Mama?" The pleading of the three younger Harris boys prevailed.

School was let out for two days since Miss Irvin, the fill-in school teacher from Eulogy, had influenza. "I ain't gladsome th' teacher's sick," Alan whispered, "but I'm powerful glad to have extry fishin' time."

The day got off to a late start after the merriment of the night before, and Martha served her breakfast of flapjacks and molasses in stages as each group of sleepy faces appeared. Had it been a school day, Effie's absence would have been discovered hours earlier.

"Yore party was shore a success, Martha," Henry congratulated. "Ever'body went home full an' happy. I jest can't figger fer th' life o' me where that ice cream freezer went, though."

"Couldn't'a rolled away er blowed away. It'd'a had

to jump right outta th' tub first!"

"Hadn't thought'a that, Martha. I did leave it settin' in th' tub all right. Th' freezer left an' th' tub stayed put. Now hain't that th' strangest coincident?"

"I ain't figgerin' it's no coincident, Henry. I 'spect it'll show up somewhere sensible, then you'll remember puttin' it there yoreself."

"No, Martha, not less'n I'm plumb slippin' a cog. An' 'tis powerful hard convincin' myself I'm that balmy jest yet. I know fer sure I didn't move that freezer nowhere."

The boys hurried through their meal. "It's jest a fishbitin' sort o' day, Mama," Alan said, excitement tingeing his voice. "Hurry an' fetch th' cane poles, Chester."

"Effie ain't never slept so late. I guess we plumb tired her out with th' birthday doin's, Henry," Martha said. "Ever'body's up an' about but her." She covered the flapjack dough with a wet cheesecloth.

"Leave 'er rest, Martha. She'll get up by 'n by. Jest be glad school's let out so she can rest 'erself."

But when Effie had not stirred by midmorning, Martha became concerned. "D'ya 'spose she's sick, Henry?" she worried aloud.

"Might not hurt none to check an' see."

Martha tiptoed to Effie's door and listened, but heard no movement. "Effie," she whispered gently, but got no response. She cautiously turned the doorknob, finding that the door was latched on the inside. She called louder, but still got no answer. Then she knocked boldly.

"I can't rouse 'er, Henry. Go 'round to her winder an' see if'n she's all right." Fear clawed at Martha's throat. *What if Effie has gone to sleep. . .never to awake?* she worried. A mourning dove cooed in the distance, its

40

minor note sending a shiver up Martha's spine.

Henry found Effie's window wide open, but when he looked inside, his heart leaped crazily. The bed was unmade and Effie was gone. In his confusion, the footprints below the window made by the ragged leather soles of stolen boots escaped his notice. He crawled in the opening and unlocked the door for Martha, who turned ashy white at the sight of the empty bed and clutched the footboard for support.

"Where. . .where is she?"

"Now jest be calm, Martha." Henry's bravery was all on the surface. "Maybe she climbed out th' winder an' went fer a little walk. After all, she's sixteen."

"Henry, you know she couldn't'a got out that winder all by 'erself."

"Did you ask Dessie?"

"Dessie! Come quick!"

Dessie came hastily, hairbrush in hand, hair askew. "What's ailin', Mama?"

"Do you know anything about Effie?"

"No, ma'am. Why?"

"She's gone from her room. You didn't help her out th' winder, did you?"

"I hain't seen her since last night." Dessie's expressive eyes widened with fright. "When. . . ?" She walked to Effie's dressing table and found the smeared note. "What's this?" Dessie held up the dirty, wrinkled scrap of paper with dismay.

"Read it quick!" demanded Martha, a tremor attacking her limbs.

It read:

41

> *Your girl has been kidnapped. You can get her*
> *back alive by putting one thousand dollars under*
> *a rock in the southwest corner of the cemetery in*
> *the next twelve hours. But if you tell the sheriff or*
> *anybody else we will kill her. This note is not a*
> *hoax. Try us and see.*

Martha slumped onto the bed and began to cry, send-ing forth a pitiful sob of despair. "Oh, Effie. . .Effie. . ."

"It's not anybody's handwritin' that you recognize, is it, Dessie?" Henry asked, trying to hold himself together and think what to do next. He knew panic would solve nothing.

"No, Papa. I've never seen handwritin' like this afore. Whoever it is ain't known to us."

"But whoever it is, is bound to know about Effie's money."

"Maybe someone in connection with th' bank. . .or th' carpenters?"

"I doubt it, but I jest don't know. I'll. . .have to go into Meridian today an' try to get th' money. Th' note ain't no joke. Whatever you do, Dessie, don't say one word to nobody. Effie's life is at stake. Do you understand?"

"Yes, sir."

"Couldn't we tell th' p-parson?" sobbed Martha. "To p-pray?"

"Absolutely *nobody*, Martha." Henry's words were tight and firm.

"Except God."

"We'd better all get busy tellin' Him. I. . .we. . .I'm afraid this is serious."

While Martha and Dessie sent earnest pleas heavenward, Henry rummaged frantically in his chiffonier for his dress shirt, thinking disconnected thoughts. *How long has Effie been gone? How many hours do I have left? Is she hurt? Or dead? Who would dare kidnap a bent-winged angel?*

Martha and Dessie were still praying when Henry, dressed in his black serge suit, grabbed his hat and left for the County Bank, racing time, praying as he went and talking to his horse.

Sarah came, bringing young Michael, after her late morning meal. One look at Martha and Dessie, who knelt in the parlor, put her to questioning.

"What's wrong, Dessie?"

Dessie shrugged.

"Stop crying and tell me, Dessie." Sarah was curt.

"Uh. . .Mama don't feel good," Dessie sidestepped the problem to the best of her ability. Henry had warned her to confide in no one, and that included Sarah.

"Mama!" Sarah exclaimed solicitously. "Is there anything I can do for you?" Martha shook her head sadly, choking on her single word. "No."

"Is it. . .another stroke?" Again Martha shook her head, a tortured look in her dull blue-gray eyes.

"Please. . .take Sally and keep her for me today." Martha's whisper was almost inaudible.

"Has Mama's stomach been upset, Dessie?" pressed Sarah. "Does she have a fever?"

"I dunno." Dessie shrugged again.

"I'll make her some strong tea."

"I. . .don't want anything, Sarah."

"Where's Papa, Dessie?"

"Gone to town."

43

"For th' doctor?"

Dessie hunched her shoulders in a half shrug, but didn't answer, annoying Sarah greatly. Dessie had never acted so sullen, even in her younger years of childhood rebellion. She felt an urge to shake her.

Sarah found a clean dress and stockings for Sally and hurried the little ones out the front door. "I'll be back later in the day with some broth and tea," she said crisply, out of sorts with the uncommunicative Dessie. Dessie stared after her numbly.

The next interruption was William, home from staking Bossie by the river to graze. "I saw Chester an' Arthur an' Alan at th' creek," he said cheerily. "Th' fish is bitin' like crazy! They was catchin' 'em right an' left, most as fast as they could string 'em. 'Bout got enough fer. . ." He stopped in midsentence, the deathly silence penetrating his keen senses. "Hey, what's wrong?"

"Shhhh. Mama's feelin' bad."

"Where's Papa?"

"Gone to town."

"What fer?"

"Be quiet, William. You ask too many questions. Can't you see that Mama don't feel like hearin' noise?"

"Papa didn't say nuthin' to me about goin' to town at breakfast. He should'a knowed I'd wanna go with 'im seein's I'm outta school today."

"Well, it's too late now. He's done gone. Take some biscuits an' ham to th' boys on th' creek an' tell them Mama don't feel like cookin' them no lunch. They can have a picnic t'day."

William studied Dessie, his brow furrowed. That she wanted him out of the house with no questions asked was

44

evident. But why?

Dark clouds banked in the southwest, boiling into churning thunderheads with the speed of an April shower that only the unpredictable Texas weather could produce. Martha didn't notice the gathering darkness until the first clap of thunder shook the walls.

"We must pray away th' rain, Dessie!" Martha urged. "Henry *has* to get back from th' bank with th' money. An if'n th' creek rises 'tween here an' there. . ." Martha buried her face in her hands and wept afresh, using her apron to staunch her tears.

"I'll pray that God won't let it rain, Mama."

But in spite of the desperate prayers of mother and daughter, the rain came—first in scattered drops that danced in the dust, then in great gusts, splattering wildly across the fields and meadows, a solid deluge drenching the whole countryside, turning the lowlands into a miniature lake.

"I'm afraid it's a lost cause fer Effie," Martha sighed. "Henry can't hope to get back on time in this kind o' weather, even if'n he gets acrost th' creek."

"What about Alan an' Chester an' Arthur, Mama? An' William?"

"I ain't worried 'bout them, Dessie. They'll find shelter. At th' church er someplace. They're healthy an' ablebodied. Th' one I'm frettin' 'bout is our Effie. What if'n she's somewhere out in th' storm?" More tears flowed onto the crumpled apron.

Chapter 5

Blessing in Disguise

*E*ffie's first conscious smell was that of damp earth beneath her. She stirred and tried to get up, but her hands were bound.

"Hey, Claude, she's comin' to." The deep throaty voice belonged to Spurs. "Whadda we do now?"

Claude moved to Effie's side. "Listen to me, kid. Like we told you back at yore house, if'n you make any racket, we kill you. Is that clear?"

"Y-Yes." Effie had recognized Claude from the start—and feared him.

"If'n you pipe down an' be real good, we won't harm you."

"Long as we git th' money," reminded Spurs.

"That goes without sayin'."

"What he means is," explained Spurs, as if to assure himself of the coveted money, "that if'n yore folks don't cough up a thousand dollars o' yore wealth fer th' two of us in th' next twelve hours, yore as good as dead."

"You got that much money, ain't you?" quizzed Claude, narrowing his hard brown eyes.

When Effie hesitated, he became impatient. "Answer me er we'll beat yore face in," he demanded angrily.

"Y-Yes."

"Can yore old man git it?"

"Y-Yes."

"Will he?"

"Y-Yes."

"Is twelve hours long enough fer him to git it?"

"Y-Yes."

"I told you 'twas a cake job, Spurs. We'll have th' money an' be beatin' it outta th' country afore th' sheriff knows we been here."

"Yore plumb professional, Claude."

Claude's ego swelled. "Beats workin' my fool head off."

"I'm glad you chose me as yore partner."

"When I chose you, I was dependin' on you never goin' chicken on me."

"You don't see no chicken feathers on my legs, do you?"

"Talk is cheap."

"What you want me to do?"

"We'll need one more note, Spurs. Sayin' if'n they *ever* decide to report us, we'll send somebody to settle up with 'em in a way that won't have a live-happy-ever-after endin'."

"Jest fer insurance."

Effie shuddered. She could hope for no mercy at the

hands of these outlaws whose liquor-tainted breath told the secret of their bravado. Jake Grimes had shot at Matthew once, intending to kill him, and Claude was a chip off the old block.

She turned her head to the right and caught sight of the new ice cream freezer, now depleted of its contents, and wondered vaguely what it was doing here. Hunger bore down on her stomach, temporarily outweighing her fears.

Spurs followed her eyes. "That shore was some good 'nilla ice cream," he said. "You was havin' a good party without it, though."

Effie said nothing, not knowing whether silence or conversation gave her the best advantage. Her mind still churned, trying to put everything in perspective.

"She don't talk much, Spurs," Claude spoke up. "She's pretty dense an' stutters awful."

"An' I'm pretty hungry an' awful thirsty," Spurs said, looking longingly at the empty wooden bucket lying on its side, stained with the residue of salt. "Where's th' cafe around here?"

"Ain't no cafes. This is th' backwoods."

"I tell you, I'm gettin' hungry. D'ya want *me* to faint on you fer lack o' nourishment?"

Claude gave him a withering look of disgust. "C'mon, helpless, I'll find somethin' to spoon-feed you," he taunted. "Yore sech a softy, see if'n I ever hire you again."

Spurs ignored the insult. "We gonna leave 'er here alone?" He tossed his shaggy head toward Effie.

"Why not? She ain't goin' nowhere tied like that."

"What if'n she starts yellin' an' somebody finds 'er?"

"Well now, Spurs, you ain't so dumb after all, I guess.

We'd best tie up 'er mouth with a rag jest in case, so's she can't holler. Thanks fer remindin' me. You might be worth yer pay if'n you keep that kind o' thinkin' up."

Claude removed a grimy old bandit rag from beneath his collar and wrapped it about Effie's mouth, tying it in a clumsy knot behind her head. Any noise she could manage to make now would be but a muffled echo.

"We'll be back, girlie," Spurs promised, with a wicked snort. "Jest killin' time until time to kill."

"Spurs!" Claude roared. "That's enough outta you."

Spurs made for the rotting door, which drooped on rusty hinges. He had not yet learned to cope with Claude's temperamental nature. Claude followed him, angrily banging the door shut with a mighty thud.

Effie gazed about her in bewilderment, not knowing where she was. The building, old and delapidated, was almost empty except for rubbish. A rusted stove and a tattered, mildewed mattress piled in one corner gave evidence that someone had tried to live there at one time. *Why have they brought me here?* she wondered.

The kidnapping scene, like a slow-moving drama, pieced itself into a sequence in her mind. She had been asleep, she did not know how long. It was still dark when she heard masculine voices whispering malicious plans beside her bed. The voices did not belong to any of the men in her family.

"Don't make any noise or I'll kill you," she remembered Claude Grimes threatening, and even in the blackness of the night, she knew his voice. As they pushed her out the window, she fainted and mercifully remembered no more. Now she chided herself for losing consciousness. *If I had stayed awake, I would have known how*

far they took me, she reasoned fruitlessly. *Now how will
I ever find my way back home?*

*How long will it be before someone discovers that I am
gone? How will they know what has happened to me? Ah,
yes, a ransom note. . . .* Her captors had mentioned leaving a note.

She knew that Henry would surely get the money if
the note was found. *But what if there is a communications breakdown?* Effie broke out in a cold sweat. She had
no doubts that Claude and Spurs would carry out their
death threat if the funds were not forthcoming.

Effie prayed, her voice but a muted gutteral sound.
Then, for the second time in her life, she felt lifted from
her earthly body to a higher realm. An overwhelming
peace washed over her, and she fell into a restful sleep,
imitating Daniel's nap in the lions' den.

An earsplitting crack of thunder awoke her. Torrents
of rain poured upon the old barn's broken shingles and
leaked onto the packed sod floor where she lay tied and
helpless. She realized with thankfulness that Claude and
Spurs had not returned. They were somewhere held at
bay by the storm. *Did God send the rainstorm just for me?*

A rush of footsteps, high-pitched laughter, and the
screech of the door warned her that someone was coming. She waited without trepidation. The light, now but
a dim gray, filtered in sparingly between boards.

A young man pushed his way through the entrance
into the barn's scant protection, followed by three more.
Apparently, Claude and Spurs were bringing reinforcements.

"We made it!" the first said. "But I'm soaked to th'
skin!"

Effie jerked to attention. The voice was William's. Chester, Alan, and Arthur followed him in, shaking water from their eyes and hair, making light of their predicament. "An' look at you!" Arthur pointed at Chester, his bare feet black with mud. "You look like th' tar baby!" Alan stumbled over the ice cream bucket in the semi-darkness.

"What's this?" He picked himself up. "William! It's our new ice cream freezer. What on earth is it doin' in this ole barn?"

Effie made choking sounds to attract their attention, but the cloudburst drowned out her efforts. Gradually, William's eyes adjusted to the dark interior of the building. "What's that tied up on th' floor?" he yelled above the din, moving toward the bound and gagged figure of Effie.

"Effie!" he cried, falling to his knees beside her, unfettering her hands and removing the kerchief from over her mouth. "What are you doing in this ole barn? Who. . . ?"

"Q-Quick! They'll be b-back in a few m-minutes. G-Get me out of h-here! T-Take me h-home," she urged.

"But. . .who brought you here? What happened? Are you hurt?"

"I've been k-kidnapped by C-Claude Grimes and his friend. Th-they want money. I'm not h-hurt, but I will be if P-Papa doesn't get them a th-thousand dollars t-today! They will k-kill me!"

"So that explains it!" William clinched his fists at the thoughts of Claude Grimes's crime. "I knew somethin' was amiss this mornin'. Dessie wouldn't tell me nuthin'. Mama was all pale. Now I know why Papa went to town.

Mama an' Dessie was *scared* out o' their wits!"

"H-Hurry!" begged Effie.

"They won't come back right now. It's floodin' out there. We'll swim out if'n we have to, though. We're goin' home, rain or no. Take them fish outta that gunnysack, Chester, an' let me have it to wrap Effie up in. I can carry her easy. You can dump yore fish in th' ice cream bucket an' bring it along home where it b'longs. You tote th' innerds Arthur, an' you th' crank, Alan."

"W-When Claude finds me g-gone, there'll be t-trouble."

"I've had enough o' Claude Grimes fer a lifetime! I'm ready fer Claude! An' so's Paw. I jest dare 'im to show his face. I'm fixin' up to go tell ever'body in th' whole community what he's up to—b'sides th' sheriff."

"Oh, no! Not the sh-sheriff, William. They'll k-kill. . ."

"They won't get no chance to kill nobody, Effie. We got you back afore Paw put down th' ransom money fer those rascals. An' that's all that matters. We'll take keer o' th' rest." Fury burned in William's young breast.

William wrapped Effie gently in the towsack, lifted her onto his strong shoulders, and waded a half mile of mud and water to get Effie into Martha's arms.

"It got to rainin' so hard, we couldn't fish no more, so we ran to th' ole barn fer cover," Arthur explained to Martha. "An' there we found Effie all tied up hands an' mouth."

"An' we found th' ice cream freezer, too," Chester added. "Now we know what happened to our ice cream."

Martha's weeping did not stop; she switched from tears of sorrow to tears of joy. "An' here I prayed that a storm not come," Martha sobbed to Dessie. "I thought

I knew best. An' a storm is jest what God needed to save our Effie! If'n it hadn't been fer th' rain, th' boys wouldn't'a sought shelter in th' ole barn, an' they wouldn't'a found Effie!"

"An' I thought God wasn't hearin' our prayers," confessed Dessie.

"We don't always know God's ways, Dessie. Sometimes they're a million miles from th' way we'd do things. But His ways is always fer th' best."

Chapter 6

Fruitless Search

"*I* smell fish!" Spurs turned his nose this way and that like a confused weather vane trying to adjust to a changeable wind, squinting to focus his eyes in the shadowy interior of the barn. "Phew!"

"You idiot!" barked Claude, assuming a condescending air of authority. "What you smell is rain an' lightnin' an' maybe bullfrogs."

"I may be a chowderhead, Claude, but I know what my smeller tells me."

The rain had resigned itself to light steady patter, but the sky still glowered with dark, seething clouds. The water-logged barn took on a depressing chill with the declining morning hours.

"It's gettin' plumb cold in here," Spurs complained. "What if'n th' kid takes pneumonia an' dies afore we git our money?"

"Yore more worried 'bout that money than I am, Spurs. An' it's my project. I know what I'm a doin'. If'n you had any intelligence a tall, you'd know that people don't die o' pneumonia in twelve hours. They got to take it an' get sick first. Then they can die. Takes a week sometime."

"Some fish got in this dump, somehow, Claude. Th' smell's makin' me sick to my stomach. I can't stand th' smell o' fish. Always made me. . ."

"I need to take you back to yore mammy, Spurs. I thought you was a *man* er I'd a never. . ."

"Aw, I was jest wolfin'. But could I open up th' door fer a few seconds?"

"Hep yerself."

The light from the open door cast a path of illumination across the area where the ruffians had left Effie. The place was vacant.

"Spurs!" bellowed Claude. "Th' kid has moved! Get busy an' find her. She's in here hidin' someplace. Look under ever'thing, an' behind ever'thing."

Spurs snapped to attention and rallied to the orders of his captain, scrambling over the ground inch by inch, moving the molded mattress with one hand and holding his nose with the other. A rat jumped from a pile of debris, and Spurs stumbled backward and screamed.

Instead of being angry, the unpredictable Claude laughed convulsively, holding his sides. "You'd make vaudeville, Spurs," he howled, "with th' shows you can put on."

Spurs straightened up. "'Tain't funny, Claude. Somethin' ain't addin' up in this barn. Where's that ice cream freezer that was here when we left?"

Sheer surprise wiped the grin from Claude's face. "She hid it. That little mischief hid it."

"You better be helpin' me find 'em both." The reversed role of boss and slave escaped Claude's attention, and he joined the search with a will.

"Hey, kid," Claude growled belligerently, "wherever you are in this barn, you better make some kinda noise so we can locate you er we'll whup you. . . .We know yore hidin' from us." He waited. "Get quiet, Spurs, so's I can listen."

No sound save the drizzle of rain answered Claude. "Make a sound, I say!"

"She ain't in here, Claude. I done looked ever'where."

"She has to be here, even if'n she's stone dead. She couldn't'a got loose."

"She got 'erself ontied som'how an' took th' bucket with 'er."

"She couldn't'a lifted th' bucket, Spurs. Use yore brains. She ain't strong enough to pick up no bucket. An' if'n she drug it outta here, she wouldn't'a got very fer with it."

"That's an idea."

"What's an idea?"

"If'n she tried to run away from us bucket an' all, she'll be somewhere real close by, meybe crawlin', tryin' to sneak off. You said she was a cripple. . ."

"Sure. Get yerself outside an' look around. I'll go towards th' river an' you go towards th' road. But mind you, stay outta sight o' people an' meet me back here afore very long. Don't you be tryin' to make no break an' run away. . ."

"I'll collect my bucks afore I go anywhere."

Spurs and Claude parted ways, and it was Claude who found the recent footprints of the Harris boys in the muddy soil not far from the barn. He didn't like the story the tracks told and muttered profanities under his breath. He turned back and went in search of Spurs.

Spurs slid from one hiding place to another, crouching in clumps of brush and behind tree trunks, searching for Effie as he went. Seeing him, Claude whistled softly, startling Spurs and sending him skittering away like a scared rabbit. Claude suppressed a burst of laughter.

Claude moved closer, but again Spurs bounded away in terror. The chase lasted for more than an hour. At last Claude returned to the barn, both agitated and amused. "Spurs, th' chicken feathers on yer legs er showin' now," he chuckled to himself.

Spurs eventually panted in of his own accord. "I didn't find no kid. But som'body might nigh found *me,*" he gasped, his eyes wide with fright.

"It was jest me, you oaf!" Claude said. "I trailed you all over these acres tryin' to tell you that I found fresh tracks leadin' towards this barn, an' I'm convinced somebody came an' got Effie—an th' ice cream bucket, too."

"Who'd'a knowed she was here?"

"That's what I'm tryin' to figger out. Somebody squealed on us 'bout th' note, I guess. We shouldn't'a never left 'er. It's all yore fault cause you had to have yer feedin' on schedule."

"You don't 'spose yer luck is runnin' out, do you Claude?"

"I wouldn't exactly call this a streak o' good luck, Spurs. I'm thinkin' it's you that's th' Jonah in th' boat."

"Now without th' kid fer a ransom, we won't get no money, will we? I think we'd better beat it afore th' law. . ."

"Listen to me, Spurs!" Claude's cutting tone carried no kindness. "We'll still git our money okay. I didn't come here to back down. But now it'll be trickier. I had hoped we didn't have to hurt nobody, but now I'm not so sure. We gotta do what we gotta do. I don't plan to go home empty-handed an' ask fer my job back like a beggar."

"What's yore plans now?"

"Th' man will be comin' back with th' money afore dark if'n he left this mornin'. He may've got delayed by th' rain. We'll cut 'im a little slack on account o' weather. But what we gotta do is waylay 'im an' take th' money afore he gits back here with it. Understand?"

"Got it."

"We may have to knock 'im out 'er somethin'."

"Long enough fer us to gain some distance?"

"Exactly. Yore readin' good."

"I'm thirstin', Claude."

"You done drunk up all th' grog I brought along. I didn't even take my fair share, tryin' to baby you."

"You think we could stoke up a little fire, Claude? I feel awful damp an' cold." Spurs drew his scantly fleshed legs up close to his body and shivered.

"Yore more trouble than yore worth, Spurs. I'm losin' patience with you. How old er you, anyways?"

"Eighteen."

"You told me twenty last time I asked."

"Uh. . ."

"Liar."

"You got a match, Claude?"

Claude pulled a near-empty tobacco can from his hip pocket. "Got one left, an' we may need it later."

"We could build a fire in that ole stove over there with yer match so's we'll at least be warm in this hovel." Spurs began gathering trash and stuffing it into the ancient contraption.

"That's Maw's ole stove. Use ta work pretty good."

The two dried their clothes by the fire and laid plans for the holdup. Spurs put his head on his knees and closed his bloodshot eyes.

Meanwhile, a frantic Henry Harris reached the Meridian Bank. If the banker noticed that his hands shook and he fumbled with the cash he had withdrawn, he made no mention of it.

"Looks like rain, Mr. Harris," he commented congenially.

"I hope th' sky holds back her offerin' till I get home," Henry replied nervously.

"Are you about to get that new house furnished like you want it, or is it a new buggy you're getting now?" the banker teased his preferred customer good-naturedly.

"Uh. . .er. . .this is kinda fer somethin' special. . .fer th' girl," Henry stammered, causing the embarrassed banker to wish that he had kept his jesting to himself. His customer seemed in no mood for playfulness today.

The pounding rain drove Henry to take cover in The Springs on the home side of Steele Creek. He breathed a sigh of relief. He could not afford to be cut off from Brazos Point by the swelling stream with time in such short supply. Effie's life depended on the thousand dollars he carried stuffed in the saddlebag.

The kidnappers had been smart, he had to admit. No

one would suspect any foul play when he knelt in the cemetery and stowed the money beneath a rock. A chance passerby would suppose that he merely knelt at the grave of a departed loved one in a moment of deep sentiment.

If they took Effie before daylight, he reasoned, *I have a maximum of four hours left!*

Chapter 7

Uneasy Feelings

"You can post Effie a letter now. Tell her we have a surprise for her." Joseph wiped his hands on the roller towel. "The colt is going to make it, and she's as gentle as a kitten."

Amy turned her troubled violet eyes to Joseph. "I've felt a heaviness in here all day." She placed her hand over her heart.

Joseph put a brawny arm about her. "What's bothering you, lamb?"

"I. . .don't feel good about. . .Effie."

"Now I know Cousin Grace told you that children like Effie don't live long, but Effie has more going for her than most. She's hearty, Amy. Just think of all she's been through! Let's not borrow trouble, love. Mother would send us a wire if Effie was dangerously ill."

Amy smiled. "You're right, of course, Joseph. I'm

foolish to fret. But I've been praying for her all morning, anyhow."

"It never hurts to pray."

Amy worked in her garden, and Joseph strung barbed wire for fencing during the warm afternoon hours. Neither of them saw or heard the approach of the stagecoach, still bearing the black "Collins and Harris Transport" lettering on its fading red sides, or saw the occupants alight.

Charlotte, carrying her small bundle proudly, came around the end of the house searching for Amy, who knelt among the onions, her bonneted head bent and her gloved hands intent on ridding the patch of weeds. Charlotte's "yee-hoo" brought her to her feet in a happy exclamation of greeting. Jim followed close behind his wife and child.

"Charlotte!" Amy whooped. "How good it is to see you! Let's go right into the house this minute so that I can see what you've got bundled up in that quilt! Joseph's stringing fencing, Jim. You should find him beyond the north spring."

Amy removed her gloves and rinsed her hands at the pump in the back yard, then removed her puckered sunbonnet. Charlotte followed her into the house, anxious to show off J.J. "How did you get here?" Amy asked.

"We brought the old coach Joseph used to drive."

"Jim didn't sell it?"

"He decided to mothball it for our own use. When J.J. arrived, he customized the inside to accommodate a sleeping baby. You must see it, Amy! It's almost like a little house on wheels. It's so clever!"

"That sounds like something Jim would do."

Amy held out her arms for the baby, uncovering his head. "What a darling baby!" she cooed. "He looks just like you. . .no, he looks just like Jim. Isn't it amazing how a child can look like *both* parents?"

"Jim says he favors me, and I say he favors Jim."

"What does your Indian housekeeper think about him?"

"She's spoiling him rotten. You'd think he was the first baby she'd ever seen, the way she makes over him."

Amy stationed herself in the spider rocker, gently swaying forward and backward rhythmically, crooning softly. "I'll be attached to him before the hour's out, Charlotte."

Charlotte laughed, her blue eyes glowing with maternal pride. "There is nothing in the world so wonderful as motherhood, Amy."

"Except fatherhood, according to Jim?"

"How'd you guess?"

"And being a grandmother, according to Grace? I can't believe she let you take the baby out of her sight."

"She made me promise faithfully to hurry back."

"You mean you and Jim can't stay for supper?" Amy stopped rocking abruptly, her look demanding an explanation.

"Mother is preparing an evening meal for all of us. We rode out to ask you and Joseph to come to Caprock for supper at the Inn—and to spend the night."

"I'd love it!" The rocking commenced again.

"Tell me, when have you heard from Joseph's folks— and Effie?"

"We had a letter awhile back. Matthew and Pauline are planning marriage in June. They want us to come for the wedding."

"You're going, of course?"

"That's our plan. Effie had a new house built for Joseph's folks with part of the money she inherited from Grandmother and Grandfather Franklin. Joseph and I are anxious to see it."

"Is Effie. . .well?"

"As far as we know. She's been teaching Mom Harris to read and write. Mom wrote us a letter by her own hand. Joseph was so proud he cried."

"You know, I've been thinking about Effie all day long. I. . .felt uneasy about her for some reason."

"You, too?"

"Did. . .you feel it?"

"I was troubled all morning."

"That's strange."

"Yesterday was her sixteenth birthday, you know."

"I had forgotten when her birthday was. It seems impossible she's that old. She's so tiny for her age."

"Joseph and I want to bring her back with us when we go for Matthew's wedding, but Joseph says it'll take an act of Congress to get his mother's permission. I'd like to keep her all winter and help her finish up her schooling. She'd be so much company for me out here. . .and we have a surprise for her."

"A surprise?"

"Yes. We had our first colt early this spring, and it's going to be Effie's."

"How nice! But can she ride?"

"The colt is a cripple. Bowed tendons. Joseph says it'll never be able to get around very good. Won't be able to run fast."

"But Effie will love it!"

"The filly will love Effie, too. Wait and see."

"Most ranchers shoot crippled horses."

"But Joseph isn't most ranchers."

"Thank God he isn't. I hope they'll let Effie come."

"Joseph and I are praying about it."

"I'll pray, too." Charlotte glanced about and changed the subject. "I love your house here and your beautiful furniture."

"The furniture was my mother's. Jonathan insisted that I have it. He had it shipped out by rail. It makes me feel. . .at home."

"I was going to ask after Jonathan's welfare."

"I'm trying to convince Jonathan to come out here and help Joseph for a while. I sent him a letter."

"That would be nice. Is Jonathan married?"

"I. . .haven't heard from him in some time now. He hasn't answered my last two letters. I keep fearing I'll get the news any day now."

"*Fearing?* Why Amy Harris, it's quite time the young man got himself a wife. He's near my age, and I'm twenty-six."

"The young lady he is courting isn't good for Jonathan. She's. . .not a Christian. I would be happy for my brother to get married if he'd get someone worthy of him. I fear the girl he is seeing has ulterior motives. . ."

The stamping of heavy boots on the back stoop announced the arrival of Joseph and Jim. ". . .I'd enjoy it, Jim. I'll see if it meets Amy's approval." Amy heard her husband's remark and winked at Charlotte.

While Jim introduced Joseph to his namesake, Amy excused herself to pack an overnight bag for herself and

Joseph. Joseph found her in the bedroom and laid his cheek against hers. "Do you feel better, lamb?" he asked. "Inside, I mean?"

"Yes, I feel okay now. But do you know what, Joseph?"

"What?"

"The strangest thing happened. Charlotte said she felt it, too—like something was wrong with Effie this morning. Do you suppose it's just a coincidence?"

"I'm sure Mother would let us know. . ."

"But I don't feel it at all now, Joseph. It left. Just like that. I'm not even worried anymore. I feel. . .sort of silly for ever worrying."

"I. . .felt a little unrest myself. But it wasn't this morning. It was this afternoon after we talked. And you know I'm not given to petty worries. Maybe your uneasiness rubbed off on me!"

"Was it. . .about Effie?"

"No. About Papa."

"Did you feel like he was ill—or in some kind of danger?"

"I. . .don't know."

"Did the feeling just pass off instantly, like mine did?"

"No, it's still there."

Amy reached for Joseph's hand. "Let's say a little prayer together for Papa, Joseph."

Chapter 8

Martha's Decision

"You be keerful, William," Martha warned. "We don't want you taken pris'ner."

"Don't worry 'bout me, Mama. Them thugs afoot ain't no match fer Eve. You know th' ole cowboy sayin' in th' West, 'a man without a horse is no man a tall.' I shore got th' advantage. An' unless'n Claude Grimes has got some meat on them bones since I last seen him, he'd be pore put to best me in a wrestlin' match."

Thirteen-year-old William lived in the bone and sinew of a grown man, muscled and strong. He had sprung up in the past year to a build bulkier than that of his father. He thought fast and wasted no moves in spite of the inclement weather. His father had the saddle, so he hastily put the bridle over Eve's ears and rode off bareback.

First he went to see Parson Stevens to solicit the preacher's help in protecting the endangered women.

Then he sped to the Gibsons' to draft Hank and Mr. Gibson also. Sarah, listening in the background, shooed the small children into light wraps for the trip to the Harris house.

"I knowed somethin' warn't right, Hank," she said, "but I thought Dessie was jest bein' ornery, an' now I feel forgiveness is due my part since I had hasty thoughts. Poor scared darlin'!"

Finally, drenched to the skin, William hurried Eve toward town to find Henry and alert the sheriff. Eve had been to town on emergency errands many times—for the doctor, to take messages to Matthew, or for needed supplies—and she knew her way. William wrapped himself about the dun's warm, firm body, grateful to feel the powerful muscles beneath him. He let her have her head, urging her on as fast as the storm would permit.

"To town, girl," he commanded. "Go to town. Giddy-up."

The rain did not slack until he reached the east end of The Springs' main street. Then it cascaded down in vacillating stops and starts as if it could not decide what it should do. He found Henry huddled in the refuge of the old Methodist tabernacle on the lee side, zealously guarding the saddlebags, anxiety written on his troubled face.

"Papa!"

Henry started, like a man roused from a stupor. "William Harris, what er you doin' here?"

"We found Effie, Papa! We found Effie!" William didn't realize he was crying.

"Is she. . .alive?" Henry expressed his haunting concern.

"Yes. She's in good shape. Didn't even seem scared.

She was mighty hungry, though." The back of William's overgrown hand brushed away the tears.

"Where did you find 'er?"

"In th' old Robbins barn. Claude Grimes kidnapped 'er. I guess he planned to kill 'er, but God didn't plan fer him to."

"Claude Grimes!"

"Yep. I knowed he was yeller, but I didn't know he was yeller 'nough to tie up a cripple girl that couldn't even defend 'erself. That's lemon yeller. I'd like to turn 'im a different color."

"What you meanin' by that, William?"

"I'd like to pound 'im from yeller to black 'n blue." Revenge festered in William's acrid words.

"I know exactly how you feel, Will. I feel most nigh th' same way down inside, but I have to keep remindin' myself o' th' Bible passage what says 'Vengeance is mine, I will do th' payin' back says th' Good Lord.' We gotta at least give th' Lord a chance to have th' vengeance. He don't like it a whit more'n we do, I reckon."

"That's a mighty easy verse to ferget at a time like this, Papa. I hope the Lord hurries up an' takes the chance we're givin' Him afore I beat Him to th' punch."

"How'd you go 'bout findin' Effie an' how'd you know anything 'bout th' kidnappin'? I told Dessie an' Martha not to tell ery a livin' soul."

"I didn't know. After I staked out Bossy, I went to th' river where th' boys was fishin'. Then I went home an' found Mama an' Dessie all scared out o' their wits, but I didn't know why they was actin' so hush-hush. Dessie jest said Mama wasn't feelin' up to snuff an' fer me to run along an' take some lunch to th' boys on th' creek

71

so's Mama wouldn't hafta cook. I could tell she wanted me outta th' house. I didn't know why, but I scrammed. I was shore mad that you went to town without me, though."

"Go on." Henry rubbed his hands together nervously.

"While I was deliverin' th' lunch to Alan an' Arthur an' Chester, it came a mighty gully-warsher an' we ran fer th' closest cover which was th' ole Robbins barn. We found Effie tied an' gagged, layin' on th' soppy barn floor. An' guess what else we found."

"What?"

"Th' new ice cream freezer."

"So that's who et our ice cream."

"Effie said Claude Grimes an' a skinny friend he called Spurs had went out to find 'em somethin' to eat an' would be comin' back. We got 'er out an' home while they was gone. We never seen 'em. I'm kinda glad we didn't, as mad as I was. I'm afeared I would plumb have fergot 'bout that Scripture."

"We'd best be gettin' on home, William. Claude Grimes will likely try to make trouble fer us. Do you know if'n he's armed?"

"Effie said she didn't see no gun, but 'twas dark in th' barn."

"We can't afford no chances now, Will."

"I have th' parson, Mr. Gibson, an' Hank guardin' th' house. Th' sensibl'est thang fer us to do is get th' sheriff to go with us in case we need him. Did you git th' money?"

"Right here in th' saddlebags." Henry patted the leather.

"You need to take it right back to th' bank afore we

go home."

"I can't git back acrost Steele Creek now. It's riz too high."

"Then put it in th' safe at th' Mercantile. They'll keep it fer you. Whatever you do, don't take it home."

"You have th' head o' a grown man, Will. You remind me o' Joseph when he was yore age. Yore doin' me right proud today."

William waved away the compliment. "Let's find th' sheriff, Papa. We're losin' valuable time talkin'."

Hearing the kidnap story, the sheriff insisted on preceding Henry and William to Brazos Point. "I want to go ahead in case of an ambush. When the criminals find the girl gone, they may try to waylay you for the ransom money, Mr. Harris. You two stay here for a couple of hours and give me time to scout out the land and search the old barn." The deputy rubbed his gun as if his fingers itched to use it.

"I don't thank he knows that Bible verse 'bout vengeance b'longin' to th' Lord, Papa," William whispered.

Claude sat fidgeting in the barn, agitated by Spurs' immature actions and comments. Claude had never gotten along with anybody for long, and even the imperceptive Spurs felt the bowstrings of Claude's nerves tightening. He tried to divert Claude's attention by his monotonous prattle.

"What you gonna buy with yore loot, Claude?"

"A train ticket to somewhere that I'll never have to see yore face again, Spurs. I'm sick o' you."

"I'm gonna buy a horse an' a saddle an' new boots an' silver spurs," dreamed Spurs aloud, ignoring Claude's ill-tempered remark.

Claude appeared not to hear the idle chatter. "Th' rain shore messed ever'thing up," he lashed out sullenly. "If'n it hadn't been rainin' so hard, we'd'a got back to th' barn sooner an' maybe caught th' thief stealin' our hostage an' beat 'im up."

"Meybe," Spurs said nonchalantly. "An' meybe th' rain's on our side, 'cause ain't nobody gonna git out an' put th' law on our trail in this kinda weather. You can be a pessimist if'n you want to. But me, I ain't."

Claude, a former resident of Bosque County, knew how long it would take for Henry to get to town and back. He had made the trip himself for Jake Grimes, his drunken father, on several occasions. Without benefit of a timepiece or the sun, Claude could judge time quite accurately.

After a space of sinister silence, he nudged Spurs, who had fallen asleep like a tired child by the warmth of the decrepit stove. "It's time to go, Spurs. Now pay close attention. I don't want you gettin' my orders mixed up."

"Yes, sarg," Spurs muttered sleepily, giving a stupid salute.

Claude grabbed him by the shoulders and shook him violently. "This is no joyride, Spurs. We work first, then we play later."

"Yes, sir." Spurs bolted upright, all business.

"We'll hide in th' brush alongside th' road. When it's time to charge I'll give th' signal."

"You hold him an' I'll take th' money, Claude."

"No, sir. You hold him an' *I'll* take th' money."

"But yore th' strongest. . ."

"I'm also th' smartest."

74

"Er you trustworthy, Claude?"

"Hang 'round an' see."

The sheriff rode high in his saddle, alert and cautious. Rumors of Jake Grimes's bootlegging activities in Bosque County had come to his attention three years ago, but the man had skipped the country after shooting at Matthew Harris, who came dangerously close to his still. Now Jake's son had returned to disturb the peaceful community, and the law officer relished the chance to settle the score.

Spurs heard the drumming thud of horses hooves first. "Claude!" he nudged, "Somebody's comin'."

Claude listened. "Yep," he responded excitedly, poised like a coiled snake ready to strike. "Git yerself ready."

Rider and horse rounded a bend in the road and came into view. "Remember you go first, Spurs. Spook th' horse an' throw th' man off," whispered Claude.

Spurs waited, tension mounting. A knife-like pain ran through his stomach, and he clutched it and groaned. "He won't have no gun, will he, Claude?"

"Of course not, sissy. He'll have a thousand grand, that's what he'll have."

"You sure it's th' right man?"

"Dummy, who else would it be in this kind o' weather?" Claude squinted at the strange horse, hesitating. "Got 'um a new horse since I was here."

"Now?"

"NOW!"

Spurs shot from the underbrush just as Claude saw the glint of the gun barrel and realized that the horseman was too big a man to be Henry Harris.

"Spurs!" he yelled frantically, grabbing for his accomplice's shirt. Spurs whirled and the thundering shot missed him by a fraction of an inch.

"Run fer yer life!" warned Claude, scrambling into the thick covering of bushes. "Somebody's sicked th' law on us!"

Henry and William waited the two hours and then started for home. With two miles yet to go, Henry saw a billowing column of gray smoke tailing into the afternoon sky. "Somethin's on fire, William. An' it's in th' direction o' our place. You don't s'pose Claude would'a set our house afire to carry out his threat, do you?"

"I don't think he could'a got past my men to strike th' first match."

"It's a big fire fer sure. Look at all that smoke arollin'. An' it's sure a burnin' buildin'."

"It's too fer east fer our place, Papa."

"Yore right. It's on th' Robbins place."

"Th' old barn!"

"Claude an' his friend must have tried to start a fire in there."

"Er meybe they set it afire a'purpose."

"That's possible."

"Papa!"

"What is it, William?"

"What if'n Effie was still in th' barn?"

"Them er thoughts I don't keer to ennertain, William. They leave me weak as branch water."

The sheriff met Henry at the Harris homestead. "I was right on target with my calculations, Mr. Harris. The culprits had a nice trap all set for you. I almost got one of them with my bullet, but they got away. They're probably a long ways from here by now."

"Did you search th' barn?"

"The barn was on fire when I got there."

"You don't think Effie's in any danger now?"

"Mr. Harris, there's two scared boys leaving this part of the country as fast as their legs will carry them. You can be sure they won't be back for a while."

The clouds had dissipated and a thin fingernail of moon hung in the placid sky when the sheriff took his leave, but Martha and Henry talked long into that memorable night.

"As long as Claude Grimes is loose, Henry, I'll be worried," Martha said. "He might not be back tomorrow er next week er next month, but he'll be back sooner er later. I think th' best thing fer us to do is send Effie to stay with Joseph an' Amy fer a few months till we can be sure she ain't gonna meet no harm here."

"Yore prob'ly right, Martha. When they come fer Matthew's weddin', we'll see if'n they'll consider takin' her back with 'um to th' territory fer th' time bein'."

"I'll shore miss 'er, Henry."

"I will, too, Martha, but it's fer th' best."

Chapter 9

Texas Bound

*T*he train jerked along, sounding like noisy children playing follow-the-leader, each car careening and twisting exactly as the one before it had done, each joint of the rail supplying reason for the great iron wheels to complain more loudly and the crossties to take up their monotonous echo.

"This is quite different from the last time I rode this train," Joseph smiled down at his youthful wife.

"That was when you and Effie came in because of Mom Harris's stroke?"

"Yes. And I almost developed an ulcer fearing you had closed the school and returned to Kentucky before I could get back and propose to you."

"What if I had?" Amy's laughing eyes twinkled.

"I would have come to Kentucky searching for you."

"Did you never suspect that I took the teaching job

in Brazos Point because of my love for you?"

"Never. I thought you were married to Jonathan, remember?"

"My brother! It still makes me want to laugh and cry at the same time to think about it."

"I spent a miserable year trying to forget you."

"And I spent a miserable year trying to see that you didn't!"

An occasional windmill broke the soporific vista out the curtained window. "This is a dream come true." Amy entwined her slim fingers about Joseph's massive ones, looking up into his brown eyes.

"This trip?"

"No, getting Pauline for a sister-in-law."

"I've known for five years that Matthew would marry Pauline. She was his one and only girlfriend. It seemed . . .ordained."

"It's been that long?"

"I remember when he lost his heart to her. She was fifteen and he was seventeen. I thought at first it was a passing infatuation, but it didn't take me long to see that it was for keeps. Pauline's always been graceful and beautiful. Pastor Stevens invited Matthew over to help on some church repairs one Saturday, and he stayed for dinner at the parsonage. I don't know which he fell in lóve with first—Pauline or her piano. Anyhow, she began giving him music lessons each week. He had a natural talent for the instrument, and it wasn't long before he was playing circles around her. He played his first song publicly that Christmas and almost shocked Mother right off her bench. But by this time, Pauline had captured his heart, and the piano lessons were his secondary reason for going to her house every week."

"Did you know all along that Matthew was going to be a preacher?"

"No, but I'm not surprised. Mother thought William would be the preacher of the bunch. From the time he could sit alone, he was spellbound by preaching. He would entertain us for hours mimicking the parson, word for word, with the actions thrown in for good measure. If one of us missed church, we always got a rerun of the sermon from William. Of course, he could turn out to be a preacher yet, but I doubt it. He's too much like me."

"Do you feel, Joseph, that someone has to have a definite call from God to be a preacher?"

"The old school says you can't be a preacher without a calling from God—that without that call, sermons would come from the head and not the heart, making them a sacrilege. The modernists say you can go to school and learn to preach just as you can learn any other profession. I cast my vote with the old school."

"But Matthew went to college."

"Matthew wanted to make the best of his calling. The calling came first, then the schooling. He was a quiet boy, never squandering words, and when the college offered a course in elocution, he grabbed the chance to improve his speaking ability. I don't fault him for that."

"Do you know anything about his call?"

"Not much. Mother thought that his close association with Parson Stevens bred in him a desire to be a preacher like his hero. He carried a high admiration for the pastor. But I say it was vice versa—that his calling drew him into close fellowship with the man of God. I believe this call upon his life had a bearing on his choice of Pauline as a lifetime companion. She has been reared to the profession."

"Matthew will make a good preacher."

"Yes, he will. One of Matthew's most brilliant attributes is his sincerity. He has a depth to him that few young men his age have. Sometimes I think he's too serious. I do admire him for one thing, though—if he knows what's right, he'll do it if he has to turn his back on the whole world."

"And Pauline will stand with him."

"The last time I talked to Matthew, he was disturbed because our church ignores many of the teachings of the early church in the Bible. He studied the Book of Acts quite thoroughly and concluded that we have strayed a long way from the message of salvation taught by the disciples of Jesus in the original church in Jerusalem. I'll have to admit, he has come up with some undeniable truths."

"Then why doesn't our church change?"

"Traditions die hard, Amy. Even when they are confronted with truth."

"Joseph, if our church is lacking in something, I want to know it. My soul is at stake."

"Now you sound like Matthew."

"Wouldn't you feel that way?"

"Yes."

"What's so different about our beliefs and. . .Matthew's discovery?"

"Do you remember us talking about the experience Effie received in the old woodshed?"

"Yes, I've thought about it for days."

"That same experience—Matthew calls it the Gift of

the Holy Ghost—was a teaching of the early church. Everyone received it on the Day of Pentecost. Matthew believes it's for us today. . .that it's available. . .and necessary."

"Has he received it himself?"

"He hadn't when I talked to him just before we went west, but he said he planned to have it whatever it cost him."

"Cost?"

"Not in monetary terms, Amy. He meant whatever of himself he must give—and in spite of things that might hinder. Friends, family, tradition."

"I see. Will this. . .belief of his affect his getting a pastorate?"

"I'm afraid it will. At least at first. He'll probably have to start out on his own. But eventually the good news will spread, and if lives are changed as Effie's was, he won't lack for a place to preach. Going on his own with no support may be part of the cost. But frankly, I admire him."

"I wish I understood more about it."

"I. . .there's several things I don't understand. Like the feelings we had about Effie and Papa not long ago. I kept waiting for a wire telling us one of them was bad sick, but no wire ever came."

"You and I just have a wild imagination, Joseph!" teased Amy.

"Perhaps the wilderness is affecting us."

"Perhaps. But I love our wilderness."

"And speaking of it reminds me of something else that has been nagging at my mind for several weeks now."

"What's that?"

"We're needing a school in our area. Dave Browning mentioned it last week. He said a new family with five children had staked claim on some open land to the south. Four boys and a girl in the family unit. Also there are some Indian children."

"I think a school would be a good idea."

"I. . .I was afraid you'd be the one the Brownings asked to be the teacher if we ever open up a school."

"You wouldn't want me to teach school?"

"I know it's selfishness on my part, Amy, but I'd rather have you at home with me."

"Then I won't teach."

Chapter 10

The Wedding

"*B*rother Stevens tied th' knot so hard it won't be slippin'," Dessie mused after Matthew and Pauline's ceremony.

The simple wedding took place in the church at Brazos Point with Pastor Stevens officiating in his shiny black serge suit reserved for just such occasions. Second only to the unpardonable sin of blaspheming the Holy Ghost was the sin of divorce in the parson's category of evils.

"I call all these dead in Christ as witnesses," he thundered, shaking a finger toward the headstones that could be seen through the painted windows propped open with smooth round sticks to allay the June heat inside the small building. "If aught but death part you, these will rise up in judgment against you."

Pauline, in her bustled satin dress smiled and hugged everyone, her gentle cornflower blue eyes pools of radiance. Matthew hurried her into the parson's gig, anxious to escape any possible mischief and get on the road to Cleburne for their planned honeymoon.

A festive air prevailed at the Harris place, the parlor brimming with well-wishers. Amy's former students came by to see their revered teacher, and Sarah brought her toddler for her aunt and uncle to share. The days merged into a week.

"When should we broach the subject of Effie going home with us?" Amy asked in the privacy of their room.

"The opportunity will present itself," Joseph answered sagely. "Let's not rush anything. We prayed, remember. Give God a chance to answer."

As the departure time for Joseph and Amy drew near, Martha called Joseph aside. "I need to talk to you. . . alone," she said. Joseph followed her to her room, waiting patiently for her to begin. "It's 'bout Effie," she initiated. "I need to tell you what happened, so's you'll understand."

Joseph nodded for her to continue.

"It's somethin' we don't like to think 'bout an' we don't never mention it in front of her as it's not a perty memory, but she was kidnapped from us a few weeks ago."

"Mother! Effie. . .*kidnapped?*"

"Yes. An' held fer a ransom."

"Why who would do such a thing as that. . .and her a cripple?"

"Claude Grimes an' a friend o' his'n named Spurs."

"*Claude Grimes!*"

"He stole her out th' winder th' night after her birthday an' tied 'er up in th' ole Robbins barn, leavin' us a note sayin' that if'n we didn't put a thousand dollars under a rock in th' cemetery in twelve hours an' not tell th' sheriff ner anybody, he'd kill Effie dead."

"Oh, Mother! How terrible!"

"It was worser than terrible, Joseph."

"Then what?"

"Henry went to town fer th' money. . ."

"When. . .did you say this all happened?"

"Th' next day after Effie's sixteenth birthday. 'Twould'a been th' twenty-fifth day o' April. We'd give her a big party, an' all th' neighbors was here an' th' ice cream freezer had jest walked off that night."

"They got it?"

"They did. An' et th' ice cream."

"Go on with the story."

"It came a gully-warsher that day an' th' boys was down at th' creek catchin' fish an' went runnin' to th' barn to git outta th' storm. That's when they found Effie there all tied up an' brung 'er home to me."

"Was. . .Papa in any danger that day?"

"Claude Grimes laid in wait fer 'im alongside the road in th' bushes, but William had rid into town on ole Eve an' warned 'im, an' they sent th' sheriff on ahead. He shot at one o' them, but missed. Th' barn burned to th' ground jest a few hours after William got Effie out. I shudder to think 'bout if'n he hadn't got her out when he did."

"That explains something."

"What you meanin'?"

"That's the day Amy and I had an uneasy feeling inside. Amy was worried about Effie and I was concerned for Papa. We prayed."

"We needed all th' prayers we could get, an' thank you fer prayin'. But what I wanted to ask you now is if'n there's any way possible you could take Effie home with you fer a few months. I'm worried turrible that Claude Grimes will return some day, maybe while Effie's at school, an' steal 'er away again. I jest can't rest easy thinkin' 'bout it. Obviously he knows she's got some money. An' I'm afeared fer Effie to stay here. Prob'ly you'll want time to ask Amy about takin' her, won't you?"

"I don't even need to ask, Mother. Amy and I both will be more than happy to have Effie."

"I'll miss 'er fierce, but I thought bein' as Amy was a school teacher—an' sech a good one—she could help Effie finish up her educatin' out there in th' territory an' meybe by that time Claude will have fergot 'bout his intentions o' mischief to Effie. Henry says it's fer th' best we send 'er a fer piece off."

"I think so, too."

When Effie learned the news of the long-awaited visit to the land of her nativity, her dark eyes widened with a light of joy. But as soon as it came, it faded and was gone. "B-But I can't leave until M-Matthew comes back," she insisted.

"But Matthew may be gone a whole week more an' Joseph has his ranch to keer fer," Martha reasoned.

"Th-Then I'll stay h-here," smiled Effie, with no stubbornness but a resigned air of resolution.

Effie's insistence left Amy puzzled. That Effie desperately wanted to go home with them she knew. Why, then, the sudden need to await Matthew's return?

"You want to wait and tell him and Pauline goodbye?" Amy asked solicitously.

"N-No. I want M-Matthew to b-baptize me before I leave."

"But Effie," Martha objected. "You a'ready been baptized. Don't you remember, dear? When you was twelve years old. It's been four years ago. Parson Stevens baptized you in th' creek in July of '87. I remember 'cause I wanted th' water to be th' very warmest possible so's you wouldn't get sick."

"I know," she said, "b-but not like all the p-people in the N-New T-Testament church were b-baptized. P-Peter told them h-how to do it in A-Acts, c-chapter two, v-verse thirty-eight. H-he said to b-be b-baptized in the n-name of J-Jesus."

"Why, Effie, it's all th' same. . ."

"No," Effie shook her head sweetly. "B-Brother S-Stevens didn't say no *name* when he b-baptized me. He just s-said F-Father, Son, and H-Holy Ghost, and those aren't names. Could F-Father get m-money from the b-bank without s-signing his *name,* but just writing F-Father?"

"No, Effie, but. . ."

"Then w-we sh-shouldn't get b-baptized without the name of J-Jesus. B-Besides I want to w-wear His name. I l-love it."

"But if Amy an' Joseph er in a hurry, you could be baptized when you git back."

"B-but I can't w-wait. W-What if I never get b-back?"

"Why, Effie, I'm shore you will. Claude Grimes won't know where to fetch you 'way out there in th' desert."

"I d-don't want to t-take no ch-chances with my s-soul."

"We'll wait until Matthew returns if that's Effie's wishes, Mother," offered Joseph. "I'm sure Dave Browning will see after my stock until I return. They have plenty of grass to graze on this time of the year anyhow."

"Th-Thank you, Joseph." The burden of Effie's heart seemed to lift, and the light danced again in her eyes.

"Isn't Effie a strange child?" Amy asked Joseph when they retired for the night.

"Very conscientious," agreed Joseph, "but what she said makes sense. I told you Matthew followed the Bible way to the letter. And he showed me where every single convert mentioned in the original church was baptized in the name of Jesus."

"Who changed it?"

"Some religious group changed it all up after New Testament days, Matthew says. The new practice was officially approved at a council meeting in the fourth century. He's studied it out both biblically and historically."

"Couldn't. . .someone in the territory baptize her like she wishes to be baptized?"

"Matthew says that almost no one baptizes by the apostles' formula. And we're short on parsons in the West. Anyhow, it won't hurt us to wait, Amy. Some things in life are more important than a ranch and livestock. I'd like to ask Matthew a few questions myself."

Chapter 11

An Unusual Pet

"Look at Effie and Pet, Joseph!" Amy pulled him to the window. "I wish I was an artist."

"What is Effie doing with that bucket?"

"Just wait and see."

"She's putting the handle in the colt's mouth!"

"She's teaching Pet to carry the bucket for her, Joseph. We made a rope handle for her bucket so it wouldn't hurt Pet's mouth."

"Well, if that doesn't beat anything I've ever seen!"

"She said she was going to train Pet to be useful in spite of her handicap."

"I've never seen a smarter colt."

"Or a smarter girl. We may have to start ordering extra sugar, though. She keeps a lump in her pocket for the horse at all times."

"Don't worry about the sugar. We'll get more. If a

lump of sugar makes a horse that smart—what does she plan to put in the bucket?"

"Vegetables from the garden."

Joseph threw up his hands in a gesture of despair. "Pet will have your garden trampled to shreds, love."

"No, Joseph. She's teaching the horse not to step on the plants."

"Or eat them?"

"Or eat them."

"How long has Effie been at this unique project of hers?"

"She spends every daylight hour with that pony. The two are inseparable."

"Yes, it was love at first sight."

"I knew it would be. Oh, Joseph, I'm glad you're not like most ranchers!"

"What do you mean by that, love?"

"Grace said that most ranchers would have shot the crippled filly."

Joseph cupped his hand under Amy's chin and kissed her. "You're making a special little rancher's wife yourself, lamb," he said.

Effie soon acquired a beautiful tan, and the fresh air and exercise improved her appetite. Amy's sizzling griddle cakes, along with a pitcher of thick golden cream and hot syrup, generated energy for each day's adventure. "I l-love the r-ranch!" Effie exuded.

Sometimes the bucket was filled to its tin lid with mesquite beans for Amy's mesquite bean jelly; at other times Effie gathered the scant pinon nuts. Pet always hobbled along with her, ever willing and eager to perform her wishes, nuzzling Effie lovingly. She nickered for Effie at the back door every morning, ready for the day's jaunt.

Effie daily scrubbed Pet down, not allowing a trace of mud to mar her white coat, brushing her tail and mane. "Pet would take the prize for the world's most pampered pony," Joseph teased.

"And the cleanest," added Amy.

"S-She's the most b-beautiful horse in the w-world, too," Effie challenged, proving the old adage that beauty is in the eyes of the beholder. Effie conscripted Amy to twist scraps of brightly colored ribbon into bows to be tied into the silky mane.

One midweek day Amy, dashing her dishwater out the back door, saw Effie and Pet creeping slowly and carefully across the yard. "E-Easy, Pet," Effie cautioned. "C-Carry the bucket s-softly now."

Amy waited, overcome with curiosity. "What do you have this time?" she laughed.

"C-Come and s-see."

Amy peeked into the container, but could see nothing but leaves of the valley cottonwood. "Leaves?"

"Look in the l-leaves. But c-carefully."

Amy found more than two dozen shell-blue quail eggs wrapped in the velvety leaves. "Effie! Where did you find them?"

"H-Hidden in some b-bushes."

"There's enough to make a cake! We'll surprise Joseph and make a Kentucky butter pound cake and put it up for Sunday. That's his favorite."

"Y-Yes."

On Saturday, Effie was gone all afternoon. The fruits of her labors showed up to compliment the cake the next day.

"Where did the berries come from?" Joseph asked. "They're delicious!"

"I p-picked them," Effie answered.

"You picked them?"

"Y-Yes."

"Where?"

"W-Way down below the s-south s-spring."

"Effie! However did you get that far away?"

"Pet helps m-me along. W-When I get t-tired, I l-lean on her and she h-helps me to w-walk. S-Sometimes she a-almost carries me."

What would be in the bucket each day soon became a guessing game with Amy and Joseph. Some days it would be blossoming plants to beautify the table. But there was always something. One hot July day, Effie appeared with the lid in her hand. *The bucket is empty,* Amy thought.

"I couldn't put the l-lid on this t-time," Effie explained. "I didn't w-want him to s-smother. See."

A tiny prairie chicken squatted on a nest of dry twigs. "H-his mother l-left him a-alone," she said. "Can I f-feed him?"

Amy laughed. "We'll see if he'll eat cornmeal."

"This is the happiest summer of Effie's life," Joseph told Amy. "I've never seen her so radiant." Evenings were spent in peaceful repose, and Effie contented herself with reading from Amy's generous library of books.

"I l-love it here," she told Joseph, dropping down beside him on the horsehair sofa one evening with her book. "I'd l-like to stay here f-forever. I was b-born here and I f-feel at home right h-here."

"That would sure please me and Amy."

94

"And P-Pet!"

"We'll have to find some way to smuggle Pet onto the train with you when Mother calls you back to Texas."

"Y-Yes." Effie was pensive for a long time. "J-Joseph?"

"What's on your mind, Effie? Worried about having to leave us. . .and Pet?"

"No. D-Do you think it would be p-possible for us to m-make a trip out to Los A-Angeles so I can v-visit F-Father's grave before the weather gets c-cold?"

"We might be able to arrange that, Effie."

"I w-wouldn't want to s-stay long. Because P-Pet would be l-lonesome. But I just f-feel like F-Father would want me to v-visit him. D-Does that m-make sense?"

"Well, yes. . .I guess it does."

"How l-long would it take to g-get there?"

"We could get on the train at the Lamy Station near Santa Fe and probably be to California in about three days."

"W-When could we go?"

"When do you want to go?"

"B-Before Amy s-starts me to s-school this fall."

"We'll see what we can do."

"D-Do you think Mr. B-Browning would see a-after P-Pet?"

"I'm sure he would. Pet isn't much problem. We could even take her to the stage stop and leave her there if you had rather."

"Th-That would be n-nice."

"There might be a problem, though."

"W-What?"

"Grace Browning would fall in love with Pet."

95

Effie laughed a bubbling laugh. "S-She couldn't h-help it, could she? P-Pet is so s-sweet."

That night Joseph discussed the proposed trip with Amy. "What do you think about the trip, love?"

"Would it set you back on your work too much?"

"I think I could work ahead and spare a few days. Effie doesn't want to stay long."

"Something tells me we should make the trip for Effie's sake. It could be. . .many years before she gets to come back."

"She's very sentimental. She said she felt like Charles would want her to visit his grave."

"If it would make her feel better. . ."

"Did you know that she puts fresh flowers on Rebecca's grave every day?"

"No, but I'm. . .not surprised."

Chapter 12

The Shyster

" 'Morning, Joseph." Dave Browning put aside the newspaper that had come by post the day before. "You're in early today."

"I slipped out before the gals awoke," Joseph said. "Needed a few supplies. What's the news?"

"The problem with living in this remote area is that you always get stale news," laughed Dave. "Most of this is what happened last week." He laid his weather-cracked hand on the paper.

"Well, what happened last week?"

"They're still wrangling up there at Santa Fe about statehood for us." Dave shook his head and sighed.

"And getting no closter to a settlement?"

"That's the way it seems. I don't believe any territory ever fought so hard to be admitted to the Union and had so many setbacks. It's not that there's not enough of us.

We've had a large enough population to qualify since 1850 when New Mexico first asked for admission. Idaho and Wyoming have been in the Union for almost ten years now, and New Mexico has a larger population than either of those states."

"Is it Washington or Santa Fe that's holding out?"

"You can hear anything, Joseph. We're one of the last frontiers and many big landholders are afraid statehood would mean higher taxes. Purely selfish, to be sure. Some say the whole matter is manipulated by a few politicians in Santa Fe. Others say the Union isn't eager to have us, either. Somebody up in Washington was quoted as saying they didn't want any more states until they got Kansas civilized."

"What it amounts to is we're in the United States but not of the United States."

"You're exactly right. I like that. I couldn't have put it better myself."

"How do you feel about statehood, Dave?"

"If it had been left up to me, we'd have been in the Union years ago, taxes or no taxes."

"Do you feel we will eventually be a state?"

"Oh, yes. I'm confident we will. It may be several years yet, though, at the rate we're going."

"If enough of us got together, couldn't we vote ourselves in by simple majority?"

"Joseph, you're naive. Voting in New Mexico is a joke. Have you ever heard of stuffing the ballot box?"

"No. What's that?"

"There are stories floating around about ranchers voting all their sheep when an issue is in doubt."

"I. . .don't like politics."

"You're from a state that has been in the Union for nearly half a century. They've already ironed out many of their early problems. The politics of our territory are probably little better or little worse than the rest of the untamed West."

Joseph glanced at the folded newspaper, ablaze with blaring headlines. "Things are happening so fast in our world, it makes my head swim."

"Yes. Governor Wallace—one of the best governors we ever had in my estimation—arrived here in a bone-breaking horse-drawn buckboard. It took him two days to cover the last hundred and thirty miles to the capital. Three years later he left by rail in a comfortable Santa Fe Pullman car. Now that's what I call progress."

"You don't think our land is in danger of being confiscated when we become a state, do you?"

"Quite the contrary. Our land is in more danger if we remain a territory. . ."

The door of the inn opened abruptly and two men walked in, amusingly diverse in appearance and character. Dave arose to shake hands with the travelers. "Coffee?" he asked.

"Coffee," the older man said curtly, removing his black felt derby and straightening his silky black bow tie importantly. "Coffee, Manuel?" he asked, his long drooping mustache twitching as his mouth moved.

The younger man simply nodded, his swarthy face set in a sort of grimace as if he performed a distasteful task. He would have been quite handsome, Joseph decided, had he worn a more pleasing countenance.

Joseph studied both men. The younger was obviously employed by the older, a liveryman for the chartered coach perhaps. His Spanish heritage was evident in his dress that included a close-fitted sleeved jacket with a vest, buckskin leggings and moccasins. The most impressive item of his dress was a brightly colored belt.

The dark man never removed his hat, a low-crown, wide brim covering held in place by a chin band. He didn't speak a word but turned his jet black eyes, half closed, to the wall and waited.

The older man held himself proudly erect, his shifty brown eyes revealing no friendliness. His presence, like an evil thing, made Joseph shift uneasily in his chair.

"Are you getting a lot of nesters in these parts?" he asked Dave Browning cagily.

"We're a pretty isolated area, I'm afraid," Dave answered carefully, measuring his words. "We don't attract settlers like the area out around Duke City."

"How's the land for productivity? Anybody taken up any government land grants for ranching in these parts?"

"I. . ." Joseph started, but Dave shot him a look of warning and cut him off with his own volume of hurried conversation.

"The last family of seven that moved south of here are hitting it rough. Living in a dugout and eating jack rabbit stew mostly. I don't think they'll make it through the winter in this desert. I expect they'll head back east."

"What about north and west of here? Any good land there?"

"My land. . ." Joseph offered again when the geographical location of his property was pinpointed, but again Dave outtalked him.

"This young man's uncle squatted on the place for more than four years," Dave gestured toward Joseph.

"Had all kinds of trouble. Cattle and horses died. I've been here more than twenty years myself. I haven't made my living off the land. This stagehouse has prospered me."

"This young man took over the land you spoke of?"

"Joseph Harris. Yes. Sentimental. Family burial plot on the property. Few people would be interested in purchasing a graveyard."

"How many acres does the grant include?" the man pressed.

"I have. . ." Joseph started innocently.

"Joseph married a girl from back East that had an inheritance," Dave subtly sidetracked the talkative guest. "And she's a schoolteacher. They have several advantages; they can make it here even if nobody else could."

Joseph was disturbed at Dave for bringing Amy into the conversation—as if he could not make a living on the ranch without using her resources as a crutch. He felt it his responsibility to set the record straight. He couldn't have this obnoxious man thinking he was incapable of supporting his wife and making a living on his own land.

"But we. . ." he objected.

Dave signaled him to silence and turned back to the hawk-eyed man. "Sir, if you find anyone in your travels that wants to stake claim on land in New Mexico, you might remind them of the water shortage. Without water, the richest lands, or even gold mines, are useless. You'd better check on property around the San Juan Valley. That San Juan River has about seventy per cent of the surface water to be found in our whole territory."

The visitor snatched the narrow brim of his dome-shaped hat, slapping a silver piece impatiently onto the table as payment for the coffee. "I heard there was some good land around here," he thundered, "and all I find is somebody's personal cemetery."

He stalked out, followed by the stone-faced Manuel, who had said not a word during the entire duration. "Back to Santa Fe!" he ordered gruffly.

When the door closed behind the receding couple, Joseph looked at Dave Browning, both hurt and puzzled. Dave had cut him off every time he tried to defend the merits of his land. In fact, Dave had purposely downgraded the ranch when he knew it was the finest in the area. Joseph wanted to let the "city slicker" know that among the arid ruins of this howling wilderness lay an oasis fed by springs and hugged by an arroyo, and that he personally was the contented owner of that prize piece of property. And Dave Browning had treated him as if he had no tongue.

Dave read the message in Joseph's questioning eyes. "Joseph," he said, his voice clad in gentle reproof, "I just saved your land."

"I'm afraid I. . .don't understand."

"Jim warned me about this silver-tongued lawyer. I had been expecting a visit from him. He goes out and finds the best ranchland in the territory and then looks up the deeds to that property. He specializes in the legal aspect of the paperwork, professing himself to be an expert on land grants. He finds 'errors' and ends up with the property in his own hands. He has made himself one of the largest landowners in New Mexico through his unprofessional conduct. And believe me, he could have found something to question in your papers since Charles, the original staker, is dead."

"Dave. . .how can I thank you enough?"

"Thanks isn't necessary. Just be careful about volunteering information to a stranger. Any stranger. Don't trust anyone you don't know. It was a mighty close call today."

"You don't think. . .he'll be back?"

"I don't think so. Having Rebecca's grave on the land probably saved you."

"Rebecca would be glad to know she saved our land." Joseph bowed his head in silence, offering a brief prayer of thanksgiving. Then he changed the subject. "Effie wants to make a trip to Los Angeles to visit Charles's grave. Do you think it would be safe for us to go?"

"I don't know why not."

"Amy feels we should take her. The problem is the crippled horse. If we left Pet alone and anything happened to her, I'm afraid Effie would grieve herself sick. We wondered if we could bring Pet into the kennels here and leave her. . ."

"Sure Joseph. Of course, Grace may get attached to the animal and not want to return her to her rightful owner. She's bad about that!"

"That's what I told Effie. Effie doesn't want to be gone from the horse long, so we'll probably only be gone a couple of weeks at the most. She wants to go before she and Amy start her schooling this fall."

"We'll see that Pet has good care. . .and I'll try to see that no one discovers your worthless land while you're gone!"

Joseph grinned. "No one but a fool sentimentalist like me would want a family cemetery anyhow."

Chapter 13

Arbor Meetin'

"*G*uess what, Dessie?" Chester found Dessie in the wash house, putting the clothes through the last tub of rinse water, which was tinged with bluing. He liked to run his hands through the blue water, pretending it was the ocean, bringing a get-your-dirty-hands-out-of-my-rinse-water scolding from Dessie.

With sleeves rolled to her elbows, Dessie plunged her arms deep into the tub, pumping the linens up and down in the cold water. Chester didn't wait for an answer to his guessing game. "They're puttin' a brush arbor up fer a protracted meetin' acrost from th' church!"

"Really?" Dessie fed the white muslin sheets into the wringer one by one, turning the crank.

"Honest to goodness. William said."

Ten-year-old Chester followed Dessie to the clothes-line, chattering nonstop. "We'll have someplace to go ever' night. Won't that be dandy?"

"Uh-huh." She pulled a pillow slip from the basket, holding a clothespin in her mouth.

"Mama said tell you supper's 'bout ready. We're waitin' on Papa to git home. He's helpin' put up th' arbor."

The smell of onions and potatoes floated from the open back door, while the delicious aroma of freshly baked gingerbread strove for recognition amid the potpourri of smells.

The crunch of buggy wheels on the double-rutted road a hand's turn away caught Chester's attention. "Here comes Papa now."

Table conversation centered around the annual event. "Are they gettin' a special preacher fer th' meetin' this year?" Dessie asked Henry.

"Yes, an evangelist outta Louisiana," Henry answered. "Parsons by name. Thought it a coincident-like fer a preacher to be named Parsons. Comes from a long line o' parsons most likely."

"Is he young er old?"

"She means is he fiery er will he put us to sleep?" giggled Chester.

"Middlin'," Henry answered. "Has a teenage son what plays th' geetar real fancy they say."

Martha cast a sidewise glance at Dessie, who was careful to keep her eyes on her bowl of soup. She had never had a beau, and by the time Sarah was her age she was already married!

"Dessie'll be wantin' to go early an' stay late," teased William. Dessie blushed beneath her sun-bronzed cheeks but made no comment.

"I wish th' meetin' was startin' tonight," Alan said.

"We're hopin' to have things fixed so's we can commence tomorrow night," Henry told him. "But I don't know why you're so anxious. You never stay awake fer th' last amen."

The weather was perfect for a midsummer revival. The morning following Chester's announcement, Dessie slipped down the wooded path to check on the progress of the workmen, hoping to catch a glimpse of the famous guitar player but staying out of sight behind a barricade of cedars. Willing hands were at work dragging up shrubbery for the shelter, setting posts, accumulating piles of leafy branches for the arbor's top, and hanging lanterns by their wire handles.

She made another check in the afternoon and found the crew constructing a crude platform, scattering sawdust, and moving in a piano. It began to look churchy and a tingle of excitement ran the full length of her body. Wooden benches were hauled from the church across the road, with the mourner's bench taking the center front position. As of yet Dessie had seen no trace of the traveling preacher's son. She would have to wait until the night service.

Dessie appeared at the early evening meal with freshly washed hair piled in dark honey-colored curls atop her head. Her newest calico dress was meticulously starched and ironed with the flat black sadiron. "Yore mighty dressed up, Dessie," William commented. "Ain't you gettin' a little vain?"

"This is my reg'lar church dress," she countered but flushed nonetheless.

"But you don't always put up yer hair so growny,"

107

William returned.

Church began at dark, whatever time that happened to be. The Harris family always sat near the front. "I like to be under th' spout where th' glory comes out," Henry parroted a phrase he had heard.

The black June bugs, as well as a few dark gray blister bugs, had already discovered the swinging lanterns. Howdy-dos were being said. Almost everybody knew everybody else.

While families milled about visiting, Arthur swung around and around a cedar post, scratching his bare arms on the bark, immune to Dessie's embarrassed sisterly glances.

Then Dessie saw him. The young man strode toward the front, a round-hole guitar under his arm. His head seemed dangerously close to the arbor's roof, the top of his six-foot-two frame almost striking the lanterns as he made his way to the platform where a splintery bench had been placed for the musicians. His slicked-down black hair had one deep wave in the front, his quick, dark eyes missed nothing, and a hint of a cleft in his chin added to his masculine charm. He took Dessie's attention—and heart—with him as he moved about easily, striking a note on the piano to tune the strings of his instrument. Dessie's heart turned cartwheels. The sermon was wasted on her.

"How'd you like th' geetar player, Dessie?" William pried on the way home.

Dessie looked up at the stars, spangled throughout the universe. A falling star tailed a white path across the sky like a chalk mark across a blackboard quickly erased. The moon was half through her nightly watch, and Dessie smiled to herself. "What's his name?"

108

"His name is Nathan. An' he asked me what your name was an' how old you was."

"William Paul Harris, he did *not!*"

"He did so, an' I tole him you was fifteen."

"William!" Dessie cried in anguish. "I'm not fifteen, I'm *sixteen!*"

"Oh, fer cryin' out loud. One measly year couldn't make that much difference. I'll tell him tomorrow night. . ."

"You'll do no sech. You'll keep yore trap shut an' not mess things up no worser!"

William ignored Dessie's outburst.

"Nathan Parsons is seventeen. Jest right fer you. Shore can make that geetar talk. I was thankin' on havin' Mama ask 'em to dinner so us'ns could git better acquainted. . ."

Dessie went directly to her room, calling a hasty good night, more pleased than upset with William. Romantic thoughts, warm and comforting, occupied her mind. She reconstructed the highlights of the meeting, dwelling long on the brief moment the young man had glanced her direction and smiled.

But alas, the match was not to be. Before the revival had sung and clapped its way into the third night, a wire came from Louisiana revealing a family illness that took evangelist and son hurriedly back to the land of their beginnings. Dessie was left holding an empty memory of a handsome guitar player.

"What they gonna do 'bout th' meetin', Henry?" Martha worried. "They can't hardly shut it down. It's done been announced an' wagons er comin' in from all 'round."

"I think Matthew's gonna fill in fer a few nights, Martha."

109

"Why, how nice, Henry!" She hugged the idea to herself surreptitiously. "I'm sure Matthew'll do a right good job." Martha's motherly pride ran rampant.

Trouble raged from the onset, however. Word got around that Pastor Stevens was favoring his son-in-law, and others said a prophet was without honor in his own country. To add to the controversy, Matthew refused to compromise his convictions, and after his first sermon revealed his new-found truths, he was branded a heretic by some of the charter members.

"I ain't never heared sech teachin's," rumbled Sister Myrt, the antiquated church organist, who had held a grudge against Matthew since his childhood days when she felt threatened by his extraordinary musical talent. "Why, speakin' in them tongues was jest fer th' twelve of Christ's disciples."

"But Myrt," argued her neighbor, Mr. Rogers, an unprofessing churchgoer with a professing wife, who loved nothing better than to contradict the self-righteous Myrt, "On th' day o' Pentecost, there was a hundred an' twenty got th' speakin' in tongues Holy Ghost. That's shore more'n twelve if I count right."

"That was in *Bible* times."

"Brother Matthew Harris read right out o' th' Good Book where th' promise is to you, yore chillen', an' all them afer off. Seems to me that includes 'bout ever'body."

"I still don't b'lieve in no sech doin's. We ain't never had sech doctrines preached in our church."

"I don't 'spect nobody can say 'tain't fer us today if'n they's people actually gettin' it."

"It's pure heresy."

"Only them that's got it has any right to say what

it 'tis er 'tain't. An' Brother Matthew's got it hisself. An' I'm here to tell you, he's a Christian young man if'n I ever seen one, godly an' upright. You can know a tree by th' fruit it bears. I'm fer 'im all th' way!"

Mr. Rogers found his way to the mourner's bench and received the Gift of the Holy Ghost for himself before dissension shut the brush arbor meeting down. No one could deny the change in the old gentleman's life. He threw away his tobacco, a habit with a thirty-year root, and not another swear word escaped his lips. "'Tis real!" he shouted in Sister Myrt's ear, but her look spoke volumes of unbelief.

Matthew suffered a time of severe soul-searching as the church members took sides in regards to the Acts experience. The Harrises stood with their son, but the Gibsons questioned his rights to contest the dogma of the established church in Brazos Point. Parson Stevens, unwilling to lose members, tried to remain neutral, a hard task indeed when confronted with Matthew's scriptural proofs and Mr. Rogers' exceeding joy in telling what God had done for him. That Mr. Rogers had received a genuine change of heart was undeniable. The parson asked for time to study the matter more thoroughly. The offended Myrt threatened a boycott.

"Pauline, I don't know what work the Lord has for me, but it isn't here," Matthew told his bride. "In fact, I. . .don't know what or where it is. We have no funds or denominational backing."

"God will show us what He wants us to do, sweetheart," she smiled bravely. "In the meantime, we'll just wait for His instructions. I didn't expect things to be. . .easy. The Lord will provide."

111

Chapter 14

Railroad West

"*I*f you watch, you might see some camels," Joseph told Effie, who had parted the curtains and pressed her nose against the Pullman's window.

"*C-Camels?*"

"Yes. The American Army brought in a load of camels back in 1855. I think there's still a few roaming around. I don't know whether they're the kind with one hump or two."

"Joseph's teasing you, Effie," Amy laughed. "Don't you let him pull your leg."

"I'm serious," vowed Joseph. "It was an experiment. I read about it in one of Dave's periodicals. Camels can live on almost anything for food, travel for hours without water, and can tolerate extremely hot weather. Most of our territory falls into that category, so they thought the camels might solve a transporation problem for us."

"Did the e-experiment w-work?"

"No."

"W-Why not?"

"There were two main problems, the publication said. The fine sharp gravel of our desert roads was too hard on their tender feet. Camels are barefooted animals. And besides that, they frightened the mules."

Effie laughed. "F-Frightened the mules?"

"Yes. The mules brayed in terror when they saw a camel coming. I guess they knew camels didn't belong here."

"But th-there's still some c-camels here?"

"A few."

"Th-They just t-turned them l-loose?"

"What they didn't sell to circuses or the mining companies."

"O-Oh. I h-hope I see one."

And so she watched, amazed that she seemed to be sitting still while the earth and its objects outside the box on churning wheels moved at a dizzy pace.

Small communities, not large enough to be called villages, and villages not yet ripe for township whipped dangerously close to the thick window. Curious children, ever fascinated by the jerking and faltering contraption on the track, ran to wave at the engineer and passengers. Effie waved her uncooperative hand to them.

The ragged backs of houses with dilapidated porches needing repair, tall church steeples, and crude shelters for animals made up the diverse panorama. Occasionally a deserted road bisected the railway.

The locomotive strained on steep uphill grades and rolled leisurely downhill, leaving Sun Valley behind, chug-

114

ging toward the westward horizon.

"Well, what did you think of Santa Fe, Amy?"

"Charlotte and Jim can have it all. It. . .wasn't what I expected."

"It isn't like our eastern cities."

"Not at all!"

"Oldtimers call it Royal City. Claims are it's the oldest town in the United States."

"I'm convinced. I just don't understand how those wooden rafters can hold up the tons of mud caked on for the roofs of those ancient buildings."

"Many of those old structures date back to the 1600's, and they haven't caved in yet."

"The city is a paradox."

"How's that?"

"The ugly adobe houses with their grimy walls huddled together along those narrow winding streets seem . . .out of character with the vast distances and deep colors of the long purple mountain ranges."

"The place will fool you. They are really quite progressive. They even have a college for the deaf."

"I. . .just wouldn't like living in a city after knowing the raw freedom of our land. I'm. . .spoiled."

"I like your kind of spoilage," grinned Joseph impishly. "I hope you stay spoiled."

The writhing metal cars, snaking their way across the mountains, swaying first one direction and then the other, made Effie's first night aboard a miserable eight hours. Railroad bridges and road crossings gave the engineer legitimate excuse to toot the mournful whistle or clang the bell, further disturbing Effie's sleep.

She propped herself into a sitting position on her

pillows and put up the shade, looking long at the racing moon, which ran about looking for a cloud to crawl beneath. Then the tracks took a turn, sweeping the moon from view. She tired herself with watching earth's shadowy masses that had grown indistinguishable, and closed her eyes. The night seemed a week long.

Sketchy dreams threaded themselves through the pattern of dozing and being rudely awakened as she tossed and turned in her narrow curtained berth.

When Amy called her for breakfast, she wrestled with a nagging notion that something important lay just beyond the reaches of her memory. Was it lonesomeness for Pet? She finally ruled that out. She knew Grace would take good care of Pet. Was it something Charlotte had said during their brief stopover at Cristo Haven? Almost. . .almost she could reach the thing that picked at her mind.

"Did you rest well, Effie?" Amy asked.

"No-No, I d-didn't," admitted Effie, with a tired smile. "The t-train wouldn't be s-still long enough for me to sleep."

"Maybe you were too excited to sleep."

"I think it w-was the d-dreams p-partly." *There!* she thought excitedly. *That's what I have been trying to recall.*

"Bad dreams?"

"N-No. But v-very real."

"Dreams usually don't mean anything."

"B-But this one d-does. I know it d-does. W-Would you like to hear it?"

"If you'd like to tell me."

"I d-dreamed I was g-given a b-big bag of m-money and a b-big white a-angel came and t-told me that I was

116

to b-build M-Matthew a c-church with p-part of that m-money.''

"In the territory?''

"N-No. The a-angel said in The S-Springs. This is what the w-white angel s-said: 'God h-has many ch-chosen p-people in The S-Springs and s-someday a g-great revival will b-break out th-there. G-Give Matthew enough m-money to s-start a c-church there.' ''

"Effie, I've never heard of a dream like that.''

"It will c-come true. W-Wait and see.''

Amy mentioned the strange dream to Joseph. "Sometimes I don't understand Effie at all, Joseph,'' she confided. "She is so sure that her dream will come true.''

Joseph laughed. "Mother would say: 'If'n it's of God, we mustn't gainsay it—if'n it's not, it'll come to naught anyhow.' I say if Effie wants to build a church in The Springs for Matthew, and she has the money to do it, that's her privilege.''

Effie slept fitfully the second night on the Pullman. She left her shade down, closing out the moon and its antics, hoping darkness would help.

Amy heard her mumbling in her sleep, and when Amy dressed her for breakfast the next morning, she noticed dark circles around the girl's tired eyes, showing evidence of her restlessness. Effie picked at her food, eating little.

"Don't you like the food on the train, Effie?'' Joseph asked.

"I'm not v-very h-hungry.''

"Another bad night?'' Amy asked solicitously.

"Y-Yes,'' Effie sighed.

"Another dream?''

"Th-The exact s-same dream with the exact s-same

117

white a-angel that s-said the exact s-same words."

"Well now, that is most unusual, Effie, to dream the same dream twice."

Effie's eyelids drooped heavily most of the last day of the journey. "We'll soon be there, Effie," Joseph comforted. "I know you're getting tired. We'll see that you have the best bed available in Mrs. Bimski's boarding house so you can rest well. Maybe she'll have feather mattresses!"

"I'd l-like to stay in the r-room where my f-father s-stayed."

"If it's vacant, we'll see if we can arrange for just that."

"Do y-you know if Mrs. B-Bimski is still a-alive?"

"Oh, I'm sure she is. Jonathan was here just three years ago, and she was only in her fifties then and in good health. Her hotel is an old, family-owned establishment. I'm sure she's still around."

"G-Good. I want her to t-tell me e-everything she can remember a-about my f-father."

"She'll be glad to."

"It s-seems kind of s-silly to c-come all the way to C-California to visit a m-mound of dirt. F-Father isn't really h-here."

"That's right, but it sometimes comforts us to visit the grave of a loved one."

"I just felt l-like I was s-supposed to come."

Chapter 15

Unhappy Engagement

*M*arlena *will notice every detail.*

Jonathan frowned into the large beveled mirror, struggling to get his tie exactly straight, and when he had succeeded, he surveyed his general appearance with satisfaction.

The cleanshaven face that stared back at him from the glass was a handsome one with bold, daring eyes and a shock of brown hair, delightfully unruly, enhanced by bronze highlights. These features he got from the Franklin side of the family. Without vanity, he knew that he was the most sought after eligible bachelor in town. Popularity could have its drawbacks, however.

Not given to dark moods, Jonathan reproved himself for the rare depression that badgered him on an evening with such a gala agenda. Of course, only he would know that the smile he coaxed onto the surface of his face was counterfeit. Marlena would never know. As long as Marlena was pacified, she never delved deeper than the surface of anything.

The *Daily Gazette* lay on the dressing table, open to the society page. Marlena, in all her glamour, smiled up at him from the lengthy newspaper account. She gave the most elaborate annual summer parties in the community, warranting the most elaborate newspaper coverage, and each social gathering was welcomed with pride by those invited and viewed with envy by those unfortunate enough not to be invited.

Jonathan had courted the wealthy southern belle for just less than a year, so the house party would be the first one for him to escort the hostess. He looked again at his name in the paper, and his ego swelled at the thought of it. Since he inherited Grandfather Franklin's money, Marlena had "set her clock" for him (as Amy would say), but it took awhile for her to break away from her childhood sweetheart, Rudolph Gattsberg. Gattsberg still hung around in the shadows, looking dog-eyed and miserable. The lackluster gentleman had nothing in his favor but a mint of money, while Jonathan had charisma. Jonathan wondered if Rudolph was included on the guest list for tonight and felt guilty for hoping that Marlena's former beau would not be on hand.

"Nina," he called to his aged housekeeper, who had been his grandmother's cook until her death. "How do I look? Have you got your specs on?"

With motherly doting, Nina passed her loyal judgment, one of approval as always. Only Nina knew when Jonathan's smiles were forced, for few knew Jonathan Browning like Nina knew Jonathan Browning—and today the gaity was false.

Jonathan realized with maddening certainty that he was transparent to this family servant and friend. Her silent scrutiny of his face brought out his most guarded confessionals. "Do I look good enough to propose to Miss Marlena tonight, Nina?" he adjured. "After all, I'm twenty-six on my next birthday, and it's time I settle down, don't you think?"

Nina said nothing, but continued to study Jonathan, discerning his underlying low spirit.

"Well, what do you think of the idea?"

"Just be sure, Jonathan. Marriage is forever. And forever is a long time."

"Amy said almost the same thing in her last letter. But how can someone be absolutely sure?"

"If you had no money, Jonathan. . .if say, you lived on Market Street instead of Rosewood Lane, would Marlena accept your marriage proposal?"

"I'm. . .sure she wouldn't."

"Money isn't eternal. It has a way of taking wings. And even if it doesn't, it's a mighty poor foundation on which to build a relationship."

"But I'm really quite fond of Marlena as a person."

"Marriage is a two-way thoroughfare."

Nina, who evidently had not meant to say so much, turned back to her work resolutely, leaving Jonathan to the nagging of his conscience. What she said made sense, but he had to choose his road in life for himself. Marlena's charm was intoxicating. Would not a future in the magic of her witchery be one of bliss? If it was money she wanted, she would have married the Gattsberg fellow, for he had an ample supply. Why hadn't he thought of that simple argument when Nina bored holes into his soul with her look of reproof?

Marlena received Jonathan at the door of her family's estate at seven, smiling her approval, pinning a boutonniere to his lapel. Amy would not have approved of Marlena's expensive evening gown, which revealed bare white arms. Jonathan told himself that when she became his wife he would suggest that she dress more modestly, more like his mother and sister dressed for public appearances. But Marlena's dazzling smile and enchanting perfumes made him forget his misgivings—almost.

He surveyed the gathering crowd, discovering to his amazement that Marlena's gown was modest in comparison with many of the others. Skirts rustled, girls laughed garishly, and Rudolph Gattsberg bowed dotingly to all the ladies. This was the town's elite, flaunting their wealth in jewels and finery. Jonathan suddenly felt very out of place in the worldly atmosphere, webbed in a nightmare. Reared in a God-fearing home, he had never drunk alcoholic beverages of any kind. He unobtrusively refused his portion of the exclusive port wine served in crystal clear glasses with long, thin stems, noticing with chagrin that Marlena drank hers without qualms.

The wilder the party became, the more uncomfortable Jonathan grew. Marlena eventually noticed and chided him for his prudishness. "Dahling, you'll get used to my pahties," she crooned. "They'ah ahlways a rollick." Her thick accent became thicker as the alcohol reached her bloodstream, dulling her perception.

With the revelry in high gear, Jonathan lapsed into a morose silence, while Rudolph's vapid personality blossomed and his tongue loosened. Marlena moved to Jonathan's side and whispered thickly, "Dahling, when the pahty's ovah, we'll have us a talk in the pahlor theyah." Her breath smelled of wine. Then she flitted off to see that Rudolph was having a good time, her eyes unnaturally bright.

The guests dispersed at the ghastly hour of three o'clock in the morning and Jonathan was in no mood to talk, much less propose marriage as he had planned. He was, in fact, irked by Marlena's fickleness.

She led him to the parlor just off the immense front foyer and closed the door. "Now, dahling, you have to remembah that Ah must be gracious at my pahties. For the newspapahs, of course. Did you know that a reportah hid in the wings? Ah love you no less." She made her bewitching eyes wide and innocent.

"I had originally planned to set a date for our wedding tonight." Jonathan's tone was icy.

"Why, dahling! The timing is absolutely pehfect! Think of what a splash it will make in the newspapahs! An engagement after my smashing annual pahty!"

"There'll have to be some changes made if you are to become my wife. . .ever." He said it with shocking certitude.

"Of course, dahling. Anything you say. Ah'll be a lambsy."

"Your familiarity with Rudolph Gattsberg. . ."

"Theyah, theyah, dahling! You'ah just jealous, and Ah love it! Gattsberg means nothing to me. Absolutely nothing. It is simply paht of mah obligation as hostess to see that all mah guests ah recognized propahly. If you insist. . ." She put her superficial meekness to work.

"I do want to marry you, Marlena. But after giving it some consideration tonight, I feel that I need more time. I have been thinking of making a trip to New Mexico to see my sister, Amy, before I settle in to my new way of life. I haven't seen her in more than two years. She has written me two letters inviting me to the territory."

"Splendid! We could make the trip a cozy honeymoon hideaway. Ah hahdly remembah your dahling sistah and. . ."

"I. . .had planned. . ."

"Ah, yes, dahling, you just must take me with you! Ah am so excited! Think what a royal time we would have staying theyah in a grand hotel. . ."

"I don't think you'd enjoy New Mexico. There are no grand hotels where I would be going."

Marlena looked surprised. "Why, dahling, Ah'd simply love it with you along to take cayah of me. We'd look until we found a magnificent hotel, of course."

"I'm afraid you don't understand, Marlena. The houses in the territory aren't even. . .modern. We'd have to stay at the coach house."

"Theyah are no hotels anywheyah, dahling?"

"No. The rooms at the stage stop are eight-by-ten squares with a bed, a washbowl and pitcher, and a small dressing table."

"No running watah in the rooms theyah?"

"That's only one of the lesser inconveniences."

"We'll manage. The butlah and the maid could provide them."

Jonathan gave a hollow laugh. "There are no butlers and maids where I'm going. My sister doesn't even have a housekeeper. She does the housework and cooking

124

herself. New Mexico is just wilderness, simple food, and plain people."

"Oh, deah, how dead! No pahties? No dancing? Let's please stay heayah then."

"I really owe it to Amy to visit her. She's all the family I have left since our parents and grandparents died, and I feel an obligation to her."

Marlena became petulant. "Jonathan Browning, you love youah sistah moah than you love me! You dreadful boy!" She stamped her foot, and her bronze curls bounced like springs.

Jonathan softened. "No, I really do love you and want to marry you, Marlena. We can plan a grand wedding when I return. That will give you time for publicity."

"How long will you be theyah, dahling?"

"Not more than two months. I'll want to get back before bad weather sets in. How about a holiday wedding?"

Marlena became sticky sweet. "Dahling, you're a deah. Ah like that kind of talk. Ah'll have the society editah. . ."

"Let's wait about announcing the wedding in the newspaper until I get back."

"Must Ah?"

"I insist."

"But it's settled, deah. You promised to marry me, and Ah won't let you change youah mind."

"We'll make the official engagement a special occasion."

Marlena puckered her painted lips into a pout and said roguishly, "Dahling, you are so evahlasting slow, but Ah'll wait."

Jonathan Browning took his leave in the wee hours of the leaden night, an engaged man. But the happiness he anticipated was missing.

Chapter 16

The Boarding House Accident

"Charles Harris the Second!" Mrs. Bimski grabbed Joseph with a lavish motherly hug when he introduced himself. "I'd have known you as a Harris anywhere. Why, you'd pass for Charles's brother rather than his nephew any day!"

"Thanks. That's a compliment. And this is my wife, Amy."

Mrs. Bimski gave them a searching look. "A good match, if I ever saw one." Amy stepped in line for an ample hug.

"And this is Effie, Charles Harris's own daughter from Brazos Point, Texas."

"Effie! The little one he worried himself sick over?"

Effie nodded, giving Mrs. Bimski a happy, crooked smile as the proprietor wrapped her arms around the child she had shared a distraught father's concern about more than a decade ago.

"Of course, you'll be staying with me as friends," Mrs. Bimski insisted. "No, let's change that to family. I've just adopted all three of you. There'll be no charge for your lodging. I'll show you to your rooms so you can stow that luggage, and then we'll catch up on our visiting."

"Effie wanted to see the room where Charles stayed, and. . ."

"Why, it happens to be vacant right now! Mr. Strickland just moved out last week. He'd been there for a long time. In fact, only two people have had that room since Charles stayed there, and both were very good, quiet boarders, so the room won't look much different than it did when Charles rented it."

"M-May I stay in it?" Effie asked eagerly, her eyes pleading. "P-Please?"

"Why, certainly," laughed Mrs. Bimski, her jolly good humor in evidence. "And we'll put. . .let's see, what kin would he be to you?"

"B-Brother-cousin," Effie grinned.

". . .Joseph and Amy in the adjoining room. It was occupied by my oldest tenant, Mr. Sawyer, a good friend of Charles. Mr. Sawyer passed away just a few weeks ago. I'm sure glad to put somebody in those rooms, because they're too empty to suit me."

"Jonathan told me about the old-timer," Joseph said.

"He was quite a character. Insisted on wearing his outdated powdered wig till the day he passed to his eternal reward. Nobody could have talked him out of it. I think he secretly aspired to be President of the United States. He knew California history like a library and saw that everyone else knew it, too. Oh, yes, he was quite a colorful old gentleman."

"I wish I could have met him. He was about eighty?"

"Eighty-five."

"And how long did he room here?"

"More than thirty years."

"I w-want to visit F-Father's g-grave," Effie said, abruptly. "C-Can I?"

"You'll be tired from the trip today, Effie. We'll get Mrs. Bimski to go with us to the cemetery tomorrow."

"I'd l-like to go t-today p-please."

"What's the hurry, dear?" Amy asked.

"Grant the child her wishes," Mrs. Bimski insisted. "I know how she must feel. I'm guessing that's her whole reason for making the long trip out here. No need delaying years of dreams another day. We'll plan to go after lunch."

To Effie's wide-eyed wonder, woven baskets of fresh citrus fruits, cherries, and dates filled the hotel with a zesty aroma. Mrs. Bimski furnished a bounteous meal, as was her custom, but Effie hardly touched her plate. Amy noticed but said nothing. She knew Mrs. Bimski was wise to suggest the cemetery visit; Effie could sleep and eat afterwards.

"I've heard about your famous dinner rolls," Amy said, buttering one of the fluffy confections.

"Not really?"

"My brother, Jonathan, wrote me about them."

"Jonathan? Jonathan Browning was your brother?"

"Yes."

"He wished for you many times. He said you'd love the ocean."

"Yes. I must see it."

"You must."

"H-How far is the c-cemetery?" asked Effie, in an effort to hurry the slow eaters.

"It's about a mile. I'll call a taxi."

"We can just walk. . ." started Joseph.

"I'm sure you could," Mrs. Bimski smiled gently. "But Miss Effie is too tired to walk a mile. So we may as well all ride with her and keep her company."

"W-Where could I b-buy a f-flower to t-take for my f-father's grave?"

"There are pots and pots of flowers on the veranda, child. Help yourself. California has never had a flower shortage. We're a blossoming paradise out here."

Effie clutched her mixed bouquet as Joseph lifted her from the taxi and helped her through the maze of monuments to Charles's burial plot. Amy turned her head away, eyes smarting with tears, as Effie knelt at her father's grave and placed the flowers lovingly on the mound. "I came, F-Father," she said simply, obediently, as if awaiting further orders. The headstone, furnished by Mrs. Bimski, read: "To live in the lives of those we leave behind is not to die." Effie let the chiseled words etch themselves into the depths of her soul.

Then she turned to Mrs. Bimski. "I l-like the pretty s-saying you gave h-him."

"It fits Charles," Mrs. Bimski said softly. "Charles will never die. He lives on in many lives. He was. . .that kind of man."

"T-Tell me about h-him."

"Charles was here during a lawless, brawly time of California history. Things have settled down a bit now, but then it was dog eat dog, so to speak. And yet I never saw him take advantage of anyone to get ahead himself. He showed a kind, unselfish spirit always. What he got, he got honestly. He never gambled, drank, or swore. 'Just want to make good so I can return to my little girl in Texas and make a comfortable life for her,' he told me over and over again."

"I f-felt like he would w-want me to c-come here."

"He would be glad you came. He was. . .you were his pride and joy."

"But. . .he's r-really not h-here."

"No. . ."

"You have nothing left h-here that was h-his?"

"Nothing. I gave his clothes and boots to charity since I had no addresses of next-of-kin. Mr. Jonathan Browning took the papers. . ."

"He sent them to me—the land deeds and the marriage certificate," Joseph said. "I still have the marriage certificate."

"It's a r-restful place." Effie straightened up to look at the well-trimmed hedges that bordered the fence. A shy thrush sent forth a vibrant flutelike melody, sweeping the gray sadness from the atmosphere, leaving a soft trill of hope in her heart. "Th-Thank you for putting him h-here. And th-thank you, J-Joseph, for bringing me."

Back at the hotel, Effie lapsed into a fatigued silence, too exhausted to talk. Amy had never seen her so weary, her bloodshot eyes set in black circles. "The poor thing is grieving, isn't she?" Mrs. Bimski whispered to Amy.

"She has had precious little sleep since we left Caprock," Amy whispered back to Mrs. Bimski out of Effie's earshot. "She found it difficult to rest in the sleeping car. Perhaps now that she has seen Charles's grave, she can relax."

Early in the evening, Effie's head doddered. "I th-think I'll go to b-bed, if I m-may be e-excused," she said. "M-May I?"

"I think that's a good idea, Effie," laughed Joseph. "Do you think you can sleep now?"

"I feel l-like I c-could sleep f-forever," yawned Effie.

"Don't you want me to go with you to your room and turn down the covers, dear?" Amy asked.

"N-No, I c-can do it," Effie answered, bidding them good night and again hugging Mrs. Bimski for her kindness. "I want to g-go by m-myself, p-please."

She struggled to her room at the end of the long hall and opened the door. Too tired to pick up her feet properly, she tripped on the braided rug that lay beside the bed, plunging headlong against the hollow brass bedstead and striking her head with a nasty blow.

Amy heard her cry out and flew to her room on winged feet. Effie lay in an unconscious heap on the floor, pale and deathly still. In a panic, Amy called to Joseph and Mrs. Bimski. While Amy bathed Effie's face, carefully avoiding the great purple lump on her head, Mrs. Bimski hurriedly sent for the city's best doctor.

It was an hour before the physician arrived. Effie had made no effort to move or open her eyes. Amy wrung her hands and wept. "I'll blame myself for bringing her out here if anything happens," she cried.

"It could have happened anywhere, love," comforted Joseph. "Don't go blaming yourself, now. If something had happened to her at home and you *hadn't* brought her here, you would have felt worse."

The doctor examined the injured head. "I don't think

it's serious," he said. "She'll probably wake up in a few hours and be as good as new. The damage seems to be fairly superficial. Of course, with children of this kind, you can't tell. They have to fight harder than the rest of us. I'd say the greatest danger will be from a blood clot that could cause problems now or later. We can just be glad this bedstead was hollow brass," he knocked on the frame, "and not iron."

"Can you. . .give her something for pain?"

"I'm afraid not. Not with a head injury. Just keep cold packs on her head to take down the swelling. You're doing a good job. When she wakes up try to keep her awake for a few hours. In case of concussion."

Amy sat by the bed all night, with Mrs. Bimski checking every few minutes and bringing more cold rags. Joseph offered to take Amy's place, but she refused to leave Effie.

She had time for thinking. *What had it been like for Charles—a father frantically gathering funds for a child two thousand miles away, a man who had lost his wife and given up his land? And then he. . .failed and was buried in a faraway country.*

Just after daylight, Effie opened her eyes and gave Amy a wan smile. "W-Why aren't you in b-bed?" she asked reproachfully. "Th-This is m-my room!"

"You gave us all a scare!" Amy replied, her voice choked with relief.

"W-Why? I just w-went to s-sleep!"

"You went to sleep all right," Amy sighed, trying a shaky laugh. "You hit your head on the bedpost and stayed out awhile."

Effie felt her forehead. "O-Ouch."

"I'm glad to see those eyes open. I was afraid you had carried out your threat to sleep forever!"

"Oh, I c-couldn't do that! What would P-Pet do without m-me? I'm r-ready to g-go home to my P-Pet!"

Chapter 17

Sandra's Visit

"*T*his is Caprock, Ma'am," the pudgy coachman said, removing the small trunk from the rear of the stagecoach and setting it on the ground, anxious to be on his way.

The girl, small and alone, looked about, anxiety troubling her clear true eyes. She saw no town at all; just an old wooden inn stood isolated and forlorn.

"I. . .Thank you, sir."

Grace Browning heard the approach of the stagecoach and met the girl at the door, sure that she had missed her intended destination. She wondered why a young lady like this, dressed in prim and proper attire, would come to a secluded stop like Caprock. She knew this couldn't be Dessie, Joseph's younger sister, for Amy had described Dessie as having thick, heavy hair and dark eyes. This girl had hair like spun gold and eyes as blue as the ocean.

The sun had painted a tiny row of freckles across her nose.

"Come in," beckoned Grace cheerfully, seeing the apprehension in the girl's trusting eyes. "Can I help you?"

"I. . .hope so," she smiled timorously. "I'm looking for a Miss Amy. Her name would be Harris now."

"Amy and Joseph Harris live on a ranch about five miles northwest of here."

"Oh, good. . ." A bit of the strain went out of the pretty face.

"But they're not home just now. They have gone to California for a visit."

"Oh. . ." A shadow of disappointment, turning to confusion, shrouded the delicate features. "I've come a long way just to see her."

"She'll be back in a few days. They planned to stay no more than two weeks, and they've already been gone a week. Would you like to take a room and wait for her return?"

"Oh, may I please? Do you have rooms here for rent?"

"Yes. And we'd be delighted to have you. Are you a relative of Amy's, by chance?"

"No, ma'am. Miss Amy was my school teacher back in Texas. A small place called Brazos Point. I didn't get to finish out my school year there, but Miss Amy will remember me. My name is Sandra Grimes."

"I'm Grace Browning, Sandra. A distant cousin of Amy's."

"My grandparents paid my way to see Miss Amy as a graduation gift. I earned my teaching certificate the last of May. They wanted me to have a vacation before I accept a teaching position."

"You don't look old enough to be traveling alone."

"I'll be twenty before the new year. It took some persuasion to get my grandmother to agree to the trip. But I wanted to see Miss Amy so badly. . ."

"Amy will be so pleased that you came. Visitors in these parts are rare."

"Miss Amy made such an impression on my life that I could never forget her. Without her influence, I'm afraid I would have shipwrecked. I wasn't. . .a very lovely student, I'm afraid."

Grace looked at the demure maiden, who would pass for a princess, and could not imagine that she had ever been unlovely.

"I'm sure you were a model student."

Sandra laughed a lilting little laugh that rippled pleasantly. "I wish I could say that I was," she said, "but my brother and I were terrors. That's no exaggeration, and I'm not proud of our behavior. I was impudent and rebellious, acting out my frustrations against the civilized world. Poor Miss Amy caught some of my hostility. But the longer I stayed in her classroom, the more I liked her and longed to be like her."

"She'll be proud of you."

"I remember crying bitterly when we left Brazos Point. My father was running from the law, as usual. He later died in a barroom shootout. After his death, my brother, Claude, and I took different roads in life. I went to live with my grandparents in Oklahoma, and Claude turned gangster."

"What was your brother's name again?"

"Claude."

"*Claude Grimes* is your brother?"

"Yes, ma'am. He grieved my mother to her death,

and I've just learned that he is in prison in Kansas for grand larceny."

"He's. . .the same Claude Grimes that kidnapped Effie Harris?"

"Kidnapped Effie?"

"Yes. A lawless young man by that name kidnapped Effie and demanded a large ransom."

"When. . . ?"

"About three months ago."

"It must have been Claude. Did. . .he kill her?" All color drained from Sandra's lovely cheeks.

"No, she wasn't hurt at all. The three younger Harris boys happened to find her tied up in an old barn. . ."

"It must have been the barn we lived in! The Robbins barn."

". . .and took her home."

"Claude got away?"

"Yes."

"I hadn't heard about that crime. Oh, I feel so badly about it. . ."

"You can't help it, dear."

"No," sighed Sandra. "I used to suffer such guilt over Claude's wrongdoing, but I have come to realize that I cannot bear the blame for another, even my own brother. I hope Effie has no emotional scars. . ."

"Effie is living here with Joseph and Amy for the time being. Martha Harris feared for her safety back there."

"She won't have to worry about Claude anymore. He is in for years and years with no chance of parole."

"Effie is the reason Joseph and Amy went to California. She wanted to visit her father's grave there."

"Her father's grave? Did Henry Harris die?"

"No. Effie wasn't Henry and Martha's own child, you know."

"No, I didn't know. She was adopted?"

"Effie's mother and father are both dead. Effie was born right here in the territory. Her mother is buried near here and her father is laid to rest in Los Angeles. She is a niece to Henry and Martha, making her Joseph's first cousin."

"I see. And Miss Amy will be back in about a week?"

"That's their plan."

"Do you think you can put up with me for a whole week?"

"You don't look like a renegade. . .now."

Sandra's eyes danced. "I'm glad you didn't see me back then! I don't know for the life of me how Miss Amy saw beyond my tough shell when I was swaggering around in Claude's overalls, trying out all the swear words I could find."

"Amy hasn't seen you since you. . .changed?"

"No. Mother sent me to live with Grandpa, and he is a preacher. I became a Christian when I made my home with them in Oklahoma."

A sudden recollection struck Grace Browning. "You were the one they called. . . ?"

"Sonny!"

"Yes, Sonny." Grace threw back her head and laughed. "Amy *will* be proud of you."

"I don't want to be a wallflower, Mrs. Browning. A week is a long time to sit and fold my hands, and I'm not used to that. Can I. . .help out around here?"

"I might put you in charge of Effie's horse. They brought the animal here before they left. She ate a little

139

sweet feed the first few days they were gone, but I haven't been able to get her to eat a bite for the last two days. I'm worried. . ."

"I would be delighted! I owe Effie a great deal. I can't pay Claude's debt, but it would ease my conscience to do something to make up for my rudeness to Effie the short time I lived in Brazos Point. What's the horse's name?"

"Her name is Pet, and she. . .has bowed tendons and can't get along very fast."

"She refuses to eat anything?"

"She will not eat at all."

"She's probably missing Effie."

"Probably. But a week of not eating and she'll be. . .dead. If anything happens to that pony, I'm afraid Effie would grieve herself sick. The two of them have been practically inseparable since Effie came from Texas."

"My life for the animal's! May I see the horse?"

Sandra deposited her trunk in the room Grace indicated and followed Grace to the corral. The small pony cowered against the railing as far as possible from the other animals and turned her head away when Sandra attempted to pet her.

"She's a smart horse," Grace told her guest. "Effie has trained her to carry a bucket with a rope handle in her mouth. Effie fills the bucket with all sorts of things."

"How clever!"

"Mustangs are extremely intelligent."

In spite of Sandra's coaxing, the pony became even less responsive the next day, refusing the feed Sandra held in her hand.

On the third day, with Grace almost frantic, Sandra had an idea. "Mrs. Browning, could we go get that bucket you told me about—the one that Pet carries around in her mouth?''

"I can send Dave out to the place to look for it."

"The animal needs something. . .familiar."

"Do you think it would help?"

"I. . .think it would. We have nothing to lose by trying."

When David Browning returned with the bucket, Sandra took it to Pet. The pony obediently picked it up with her teeth, awaiting Sandra's orders, a transformed animal.

"Look, Mrs. Browning," Sandra beamed. "It's working!"

"Bless you!"

Sandra led the filly across the feed lot, then took the bucket from her, allowing her to eat her feed peacefully. Then the two of them went for a walk to find something to fill the empty bucket.

"What does Effie put in the bucket?" called Sandra.

"Anything from berries to cockleburs, Sandra," waved Grace. "Just so you put something in that tin can!"

Every day thereafter, Sandra and the halting white pony roamed the surrounding prairie, a lump of sugar waiting in Sandra's pocket as a reward for a job well done.

"Sandra is an answer to prayer, Dave," Grace told her husband. "She saved the life of Effie's colt."

"So you prayed too, huh?" Dave grinned. "I knew without a miracle, Pet wouldn't be here when Effie got back from California. Sandra Grimes was our miracle."

Chapter 18

A Rich Discovery!

"*A* week of bed rest," ordered the doctor, putting his instruments back into his black bag.

"But I feel g-good enough to t-travel," insisted Effie.

"Just a precautionary measure," he said.

"I w-want to go home to my h-horse."

The doctor chuckled. "You're a persistent one, but let's not take any chances."

"I've s-seen all of C-California that I want to s-see," Effie fretted to Amy. "Now I want to s-see Pet."

"Grace Browning is taking good care of Pet," Amy assured. "And you'll want to see the ocean."

"No, you go a-ahead and s-see the o-ocean," persisted Effie. "It's just w-water. As soon as the d-doctor lets me up f-from here, I want to g-go straight to the t-train station!"

Amy and Mrs. Bimski made plans for a trip to the

beach while Joseph stayed behind to look after Effie. "It's a shame to be so close and not see the beauties of the Pacific that Jonathan wrote me about," Amy reasoned and Mrs. Bimski agreed. "I'm a nature lover by birth."

Mrs. Bimski placed a basket of fresh fruit on the nightstand beside Effie's bed, and Amy kissed her still swollen forehead. "I'll tell you all about it when I get back, love," she promised.

"O-Okay."

"We'll hurry."

"No, don't r-rush."

Joseph checked on Effie twice, finding her asleep both times. The third time he went to her room, she stirred. "J-Joseph," she called drowsily.

"At your service, ma'am," he bowed teasingly.

"I wish you'd f-fix the b-bedpost. Everytime the d-door closes, it r-rattles and w-wakes me up."

Joseph looked at the brass post. "The cap is loose," he observed. "At the top joint."

"I must h-have knocked it loose when I h-hit it with my h-head."

"And it's on crooked."

"What, m-my h-head?" laughed Effie, yawning. "Th-Then th-that's why it f-feels like th-this!"

"I'd best pry it off and start over."

"V-Very carefully," Effie joked, pointing to her forehead. "I m-may need it."

Joseph smiled, glad to see Effie able to jest again. "I'll see if I can find a hammer in Mrs. Bimski's supply closet."

"Ouch," she called after him, laughing.

He found Effie munching on a plum when he returned. "Are you sure the noise I make fixing the post won't give you a headache?"

"J-Joseph, don't m-mind me. I'm w-well. It's s-silly for the d-doctor to make me s-stay in bed anyhow. P-Pound all you p-please. Just stop th-that awful r-rattle so I c-can get some s-sleep before I get back on th-that s-sleepless train!"

Joseph worked and wiggled the brass cap, which was wedged crazily into position on one side and annoyingly loose on the other. That it had had a jolting blow was evident. The rattling, however, didn't make sense. It seemed to be coming from the bedpost itself.

When the stubborn cap finally submitted to Joseph's prizing, he sat down in the wing-backed wicker chair to straighten it.

"It's hot in here."

"Uh-huh."

He opened the south window for more ventilation. A cool breeze from the sea filled the room. "That's better."

"B-Better, but not as g-good as our r-ranch air b-back home."

"I believe you're homesick, Effie."

"F-For Pet."

"I need pliers for this job." Joseph returned to the supply room. The breeze, sweeping through the open window, caught the door and closed it behind him with a bang.

Joseph searched at length, but found no pliers. "I'm not having much luck finding tools," he told Effie when he returned.

"N-Never mind," Effie said. "It isn't the b-bent c-cap that's the p-problem anyway."

"I have the cap off."

"B-But the b-bedpost r-rattled anyhow when the w-wind blew the d-door shut a-awhile ago."

"Now that is strange."

"I g-guess I b-broke s-something inside the b-bedstead when I h-hit it with my h-head."

"I'll have a look."

Joseph laid aside the brass top and peered into the hollow darkness of the post. "There is something here," he said, "and it's bumping against the metal. It seems to be a rock on top of some old stuffing."

"P-Please get it o-out so I c-can s-sleep," Effie implored patiently.

"I can't imagine who would have put a rock in there." Joseph ran his arm into the cavity to get the offending stone, bringing it to the surface between his thumb and forefinger. "But here it is."

"Th-Throw it a-away," Effie suggested. "A-And my p-problems will be o-over."

Joseph caught his breath in a sharp gasp.

"D-Did you h-hurt your arm, J-Joseph? L-let me s-see."

"No, I. . .Effie, this is no ordinary rock. It's a *gold nugget!*"

"Is it w-worth a lot?"

"An awful lot."

"H-How did it g-get there?"

"I don't know."

"We'll h-have to give it to M-Mrs. B-Bimski. It b-belongs to h-her. We f-found it in h-her house."

"Yes, of course. She'll be. . .excited."

"Y-Yes."

"A prospector must have hidden it here."

"L-Look a-again. There m-might be a-another one."

"One nugget in a lifetime is all I ever expect to see. It looks as though someone stuffed some material down below the nugget."

"L-Look under it."

Joseph laughed. "You're a hard taskmaster, Effie Harris!" But he rummaged about in the opening with his hand, dislodging the mass of fabric and sending it thudding to the bottom of the hollow post.

"W-What f-fell?"

"I don't know. It sounded like something heavy. It looks as though I'll have to dismantle this whole bed. . .and you're not supposed to be out of it."

Effie gathered her robe close about her and jumped up. "Th-The doctor w-will never k-know. H-Hurry before A-Amy gets b-back. She'll be u-upset with me for g-getting up if she c-catches me."

Joseph wrenched the headboard from the iron rails with the hammer, leaving the slats, springs, and mattress poised at a downward angle from the foot of the bed. He turned the brass post upside down and pounded on the bottom. A leather bag of gold came out top first, scattering massive nuggets across the floor and under the bed.

"Ooooh, J-Joseph!"

"Be very quiet, Effie. We don't want any of the other tenants to know this is here."

Joseph gathered the treasure, combing the surface of the floor with his hand, and quickly reassembled the framework of the bed. A combination of fright and awe gripped him.

"I-Is the b-bag plumb f-full?" whispered Effie.

"I. . .think so. It's terribly heavy. Must weigh thirty

147

pounds." Joseph plunged his fingers into the bag, feeling a crumpled piece of paper. "There's a scrap of paper. . . ."

"Oh, won't Mrs. B-Bimski be p-pleased. She'll be r-rich and won't h-have to w-work ever again."

"Yes, she'll be wealthy. This is more than enough to last her the rest of her life."

"Sh-She'll probably t-try to f-find the o-owner."

"I'm sure she will."

Joseph fumbled with the paper, smoothing it. "The paper has a message for someone. Maybe it's a clue as to who left the gold here."

"R-Read it."

"It says, 'Mrs. Bimski: All my gold bullion goes to my little daughter, Effie Harris, at Five Oaks Post in Brazos Point, Texas.' Signed: C. Harris."

"J-Joseph! You mean it was F-Father's m-money?"

"It. . .must have been." Joseph scratched his head as if to comprehend the significance of the find.

"Oh, J-Joseph, c-can I see the n-note for myself? Can I h-hold it in my o-own hands? C-Can I k-keep it b-because it's my f-father's own h-handwriting?"

Joseph gave her the note, and she stared at it briefly, trancelike. Then she closed her eyes and pressed it to her lips in an intense embrace. "M-Mrs. B-Bimski will l-let me have it, won't s-she? Th-The note means more to m-me than all the g-gold. It tells me h-how much F-Father really l-loved me!"

"I. . ." Joseph started, but the front door of the hotel opened, and he quickly hid the pouch of precious gold beneath the pillow opposite Effie.

Amy burst in, flushed and exuberant. "Effie! The

ocean is simply beautiful! It scrambles up the beach to your feet and then backs off again, frothing and foaming. . ." She stopped, looking from Effie to Joseph and back to Effie again. "What's wrong, Joseph? Is Effie. . .all right?"

Joseph signaled her to silence and she sat down, trembling. "Did you get another doctor's report, Joseph?" The look on Joseph's face was a puzzle.

"We've found something, Amy. . ."

"What is it, Joseph?"

"We found a whole poke of gold in the bedpost—that belonged to Charles."

"Why, Joseph, how can you be sure?"

Effie handed Amy the note. Her hands shook as she read it. "Oh, Joseph! Oh, Joseph! Where. . .is it?"

"Shhhh. Under the extra pillow on Effie's bed."

"We'll have to tell Mrs. Bimski, won't we? The note is addressed to her."

"Yes. Call her in, Amy. And shut the door."

Mrs. Bimski read the note, brushing away glad tears. "You can't know how happy this makes me," she cried. "Now I feel like his time out here was not. . .wasted. The day he was shot, he told me he had something he needed to discuss with me. . .but we were interrupted. I always felt that he planned to tell me where he kept his gold in case. . .anything happened to him."

"May I h-have the n-note for my v-very own to t-take h-home with me, Mrs. B-Bimski?" Effie asked the question desperately, urgently.

"Why, of course, child!"

"It m-means m-more to m-me than the g-gold."

Effie turned to Amy. "D-Do you think m-maybe God

149

g-gave me an urge to c-come here so we could f-find this?''

"I. . .think so. It would be a good enough reason. But I'm sorry you had to get such a knot on your head to find it.''

"It was w-worth it!''

"Joseph,'' Mrs. Bimski's voice was low and serious, "good men have been killed for less. No one must know about the gold. Absolutely no one.''

"No one will know, Mrs. Bimski.''

"There used to be an old saying in the West; 'It's one thing to get gold, but it's another thing to get home with it.' Consider what happened to your own uncle who spent two years of his life accumulating the cache.''

"I'll hide it in my suitcase.''

"No, that won't do. That method has a high failure rate. We'll have to think of something else.''

"I could carry it in my pockets, but the weight of it. . .''

"No. . .''

"I need to keep it with me at all times, don't I?''

"Yes.''

"Maybe I could put it in my purse, Joseph,'' Amy offered.

"It would be too heavy for you to lift, Amy.''

"I have an idea.'' Mrs. Bimski's eyes lighted up. "We'll put it in my cracker tin with a lid. If you can *pretend* it's not a bit heavy, Joseph, everyone will just think you are taking crackers along on the trip for Effie. Especially if you casually mention that she has been under a doctor's care.''

"You are indeed a wise woman, Mrs. Bimski.''

"G-Give her the b-biggest n-nugget, Joseph.''

"No, dear," objected Mrs. Bimski. "I am comfortably situated, and Charles was willing to give his life so that you might be taken care of. If the good Lord wills, you will have many years left on earth. With this money, you can be self-sufficient for a lifetime. It is enough that these old eyes of mine have seen Charles's dream come true. Invest wisely and live righteously—and God bless you."

Chapter 19

The Cracker Box

"Leaving, eh?" The gregarious driver of the horse-drawn taxi babbled on. "It's a mighty bad time to be leaving California, mister. Best thing for you to do is go home, sell all you have and give it to the poor, and come to Los Angeles. I can tell you a secret that few people know yet, mister. Oil has just been discovered right near here, and there'll be a run like the gold run. When you get home and read your Sunday paper, you'll wish you had listened to me and stayed to make your fortune."

The inattentive driver maneuvered the cart recklessly uphill and down, swerving precariously around hairpin turns. Joseph held the cracker box under his arm, grateful that Mrs. Bimski had packed it well and no telltale rattle aroused suspicion about its contents. As the buggy jounced and bumped over the uneven streets, he envisioned a sickening spill with the nuggets in the tin spreading over the entire neighborhood. Effie clung to Amy and Amy clung to Joseph. Neither saw the beauty of the flowers or the laden fruit trees.

"I. . .f-feel s-sick," Effie stuttered, her complexion taking on a greenish tint. "H-how much f-farther to the s-station?"

"Sir, could you slow this thing down?" Joseph finally suggested. "My. . .Miss Effie. . .is getting sick."

"Motion sickness," the talkative driver said nonchalantly. "If a body ain't used to these dips and curves, it affects them thataway. The faster we go, the sooner it's over with, though."

Effie closed her eyes, swept by dizziness and a sudden churning in the pit of her stomach. She laid her head against Amy's shoulder.

"Might try giving her one of those crackers from your box there," the speed demon suggested, making yet another abrupt turn that threw Effie against Amy and Amy against Joseph. "Crackers are good to settle one's stomach, you know. Maw always said there was nothing better."

"N-No, th-thanks," Effie responded, too quickly. "I c-couldn't possibly e-eat a thing right n-now. It would c-come right back u-up." She suppressed a gag.

"Smart of you to take crackers along for the train ride, mister," he kept talking nonstop. "The rocking of those rail cars does make some people nauseous. Kids and ladies, mostly. Especially on a long trip or in a high altitude. You going far, mister?"

"Yes, sir," Joseph answered, volunteering no further information.

"Too bad, too bad," taunted the driver, clucking his

tongue annoyingly. "Running away from riches! If I was your age, I'd dive in and get my share of the bucks." He removed his hat, uncovering a smooth head with just a rim of graying hair left. "When you get my age, you'll look back and wish you'd taken advantage of your opportunity."

The crowded railway station, smelling of stale pipe smoke and garments that had been stowed in mothballs, looked like heaven's portals to the terrified Harris trio. An elderly gentleman offered Effie his place on the worn bench, while a chain reaction of moving bodies made room for Amy, too.

"I'll never c-complain about a t-train ride a-again," breathed Effie with relief, some of the green fading from her pinched face.

"Nor I," laughed Amy shakily.

The line at the ticket counter was long and moved slowly. "It seems everybody is in a frenzy to get out of California today in spite of the taxi driver's sales pitch," Joseph commented. "If I don't get in line, we'll be here until next week!"

Two seedy-looking characters pushed ahead of Joseph, looking furtively this way and that. One punched the other in the ribs. "That guy's taking his food along." He gestured toward Joseph's cracker box. "He must know something we don't. Food may be lousy on this liner."

"He's probably got a good idea," the other gave a throaty chuckle. "Except I want to get out of this state with more than crackers." He winked a shifty eye. "And I can't wait until tomorrow for transportation, either. I'm renting us a private car."

"Th-The train will be f-filled up b-before Joseph

g-gets our tickets, a-and we'll have to w-wait for a-another one," observed Effie. "M-Maybe we'll have to s-sit here all n-night."

"I hope not, but it does look that way," Amy agreed, praying silently.

Joseph bought the last three vacancies on the cush-ioned coach. "We'll start out crowded," he said. "But at each station, a few will drop off. By the time we get to the state line, we'll have leg room. At least we got on."

"That's all that matters." Amy gave him a relieved smile.

The conductor gave the first call, and they boarded the train and took their seats toward the rear of the car. The weight of the cracker box fell heavily upon Joseph's arm, but from all outward appearances, a child could have carried it with ease. His imposture made Amy laugh.

The restless mass of passengers settled into a spec-trum of gray shades, with a brown hat or blue coat mak-ing itself conspicuous here and there. The wild cacophony of sound that accompanied the boarding throng eventually dissipated to a discordant hum that filled the vaulted space. The conductor came for the boarding passes. "The train has been delayed, but the problem should be solved shortly," he stated, matter-of-factly.

Ten minutes passed and still they sat in the terminal. Joseph placed the tin box between his knees to rest his arm. "A-Are we ever g-going?" Effie asked.

"Probably the train needs some minor repairs," Joseph consoled her, looking at his fob watch.

Twice more he pulled out his timepiece as thirty minutes passed, then forty-five. The coach became steamy with body heat in the rising humidity. A young woman with a small, fretful child in tow pushed her way down the narrow aisle toward the water keg.

The lad, spying Joseph's cracker box, pointed and wailed, "He has quackers. I want a quacker. I'm hungry!" Other passengers heard and snickered. The embarrassed mother hurried the child on while a red-faced Joseph turned his face toward the window, feigning inattentiveness.

Staring absently into space, Joseph caught the glint of a sheriff's badge as the officer hurried down the length of the train, apparently much agitated. He gestured wildly to someone out of sight.

The conductor appeared again. "It is requested that no one leave the train, please. And please remain seated," he said in a monotonic, recorded-cylinder voice, as he strode with crisp steps from car to car.

"What's wrong, Joseph?" Amy whispered.

"I don't know," he returned in an undertone, "I just saw an officer pass the window. Maybe it's a. . .holdup."

"Oh, no."

The conductor bustled back through. "Engine trouble, sir?" Joseph asked politely.

"No, we're under holding orders," the conductor answered curtly. "Someone is reportedly leaving the state with stolen gold, and the law enforcement officers are making a thorough search of the train before we proceed. Don't worry, this is nothing out of the ordinary for California, and we'll be on our way in an hour or so when the search is satisfactorily concluded. I'll open the ventilators for you."

Amy blanched a ghostly white, but Joseph held his mien admirably. Effie remained unperturbed by the news.

157

"We'll all be searched, won't we, Joseph?" Amy asked.

"I expect so."

She stirred restlessly. If the officers discovered the nuggets in the cracker tin, it would be Joseph Harris who would be carted off to jail until sufficient evidence proved his innocence. Effie had her note, of course, and Mrs. Bimski would be a character witness, but the time and red tape could be endless, causing them weeks of delay in returning to their ranch.

A burly policeman came into the cushion car, his nightstick bumping against his leg. The small boy hid his face in his mother's skirts and wailed the louder. "Don't let 'im get me, Mama. . .don't let 'im get me. . ."

"Shhhh," she cautioned. "He ain't after you."

"Ladies and gentlemen," the conductor announced. "This is Sergeant Thomas, an officer of the State of California and we regret to tell you that we must search through all the ladies' handbags and the men's valises for some property reportedly stolen. Then our train can proceed to its destination. We're sorry for the inconvenience."

A second policeman, young and cocky, strode into the car to assist in the process. Amy's eyes met Joseph's, and she read the flicker of alarm there, though it was imperceptible to others. He moistened his lips nervously.

Beginning at the front of the car and proceeding back, the officers worked swiftly, rummaging through purses and overnight bags, missing nothing. Scents of soap and hair oil permeated the oppressive heat as toilet articles were removed from their carrying cases in the search.

When the officers reached their section, Amy handed over her purse pleasantly. The searchers sifted through combs, brooches, handkerchiefs, a pair of stockings for Effie, writing material, sea shells from the beach, a nail file, and sundry other items. "Is there anything ladies don't carry in their handbags?" the rookie asked, and the senior officer gave him a dirty look.

The older man turned to Joseph. "Any luggage?" he asked gruffly.

"No, sir. I checked all mine on the baggage car."

"Any of your suitcases locked?"

"No, sir."

"They'll be examined there."

"That's fine with me, sir."

Then the man of angry countenance saw the cracker box sitting on the seat between Joseph's knees. "We'd best have a look in that cracker box, Jeffery."

"Aw, Sarge," the novice protested, cutting his eyes toward Effie. "It's just crackers for the little sick girl there. Let him be."

"We don't take no chances, Jeff. I've found gold hidden in mighty peculiar places in my day on the force."

Instead of lifting the box, he simply snapped off the lid to determine its secret within. Amy held her breath, expecting the worst. It would be obvious to these lawmen that Joseph was trying to conceal the gold in an unsuspicious container.

But Mrs. Bimski had thought to put crackers in the mouth of the box, thereby hiding the poke of gold. *Bless Mrs. Bimski!* Amy thought.

"Told you, Sarge," the recruit quipped, obviously trying the patience of his superior to its utmost limits. "You could see the girl is sickly if you'd looked. They been out here for their health."

The officer handed the lid back to Joseph to replace without a word and moved out through the rear door toward the caboose. Not more than ten minutes later, the man with the shifty eyes and surly mouth who had stood in front of Joseph in the ticket line was marched, along with his accomplice, from the train, handcuffed.

"Looks like they found their thief," a man across the aisle from Joseph quipped. Joseph nodded absently.

The great engine spat and sputtered, its black back turned to the sun, and then inched from the station, the clickety-clack of the wheels rising to a crescendo as the speed increased.

"At last!" Amy cheered.

"You l-look all s-spent, Amy," Effie reproached.

"Yes, love. It's been a long, hard day."

"You w-worry about unnecessary th-things."

Amy knew Effie referred to the cracker box scare.

"W-Was Joseph w-worried, too?"

"Yes, he was. Very much. It was a close call."

"Th-There was no n-need to w-worry."

Amy decided that Effie was too young or too naive to realize the value of the gold Charles had left to her.

"D-Do you remember my d-dreams on the w-way out h-here? The d-dreams that wouldn't l-leave me a-alone?"

Amy had forgotten the strange dreams. Now she tried to recall the details. . .a bag of gold. . .a white angel. . .a church for Matthew. . .

"Why, yes, now I do remember, Effie."

"S-See. That's w-why there's no n-need to w-worry. Matthew m-must have h-his church. N-Nothing will happen to k-keep him from it."

Anyone who happened to be listening would not have understood the conversation at all.

Chapter 20

Back to the Ranch

Jim and Charlotte, along with five-month-old J.J., met the train at the Lamy station. "We want to take you the rest of the way home in our 'house carriage,' " insisted Charlotte. "We nab any excuse to go to Caprock! Anyhow, we want to hear all about your trip."

"It was quite eventful," Amy laughed.

"Joseph can ride with Jim on the driver's box and visit while we enjoy the inside comforts." Charlotte looked from Amy to Joseph, espying the cracker box. "Did you bring those crackers all the way from California, Joseph?"

Joseph grinned. "Yes."

"Well, you can throw that old cracker tin away if you like," she said. "The crackers are probably stale by now. I have some fresh cakes made for us."

Joseph winked at Amy, then turned to Charlotte. "This box is sort of a keepsake from California. The lady who ran the hotel where Charles last stayed give it to me."

"Oh, I see. But it's a funny souvenir."

A pillow-lined daybed awaited Effie in the unique house coach. A canvas bag of water was mounted on the outside of the coach to keep the water cool, and a spout ran inside. Individual cakes, fruits, and finger sandwiches were packed in a compartment built just for such dainties.

"Jim is a g-genius," Effie remarked with delight, her eyes compassing the whole homey cab decorated with rich red curtains. "To t-turn a c-coach into a little h-house."

"Indeed he is," Charlotte laughed. "I told him he should get a patent from Washington on house coaches. He might get rich quick."

"I'm r-rich," Effie said abruptly. "B-But I don't f-feel any d-different."

"Yes, I'm glad Amy found you!" Charlotte said.

"She's not talking about Grandfather's estate, Charlotte. That is a small amount compared to her worth now. On this coach is enough gold to last her two lifetimes."

Charlotte's eyes grew large with surprise, then fear. "Oh. . .I hope nobody knows about it. Gold is dangerous to have out here."

"Nobody will ever suspect. It's hidden well."

"Hidden? It's not in your suitcase?"

"No. It's in that cracker box Joseph has under his arm."

Charlotte tittered. "It *is* hidden well. I thought it strange that Joseph would be so interested in an old cracker box. At last—the cracker box mystery has been solved! But where did Effie get the gold?"

"It belonged to Charles. He left it hidden in the hollow

bedpost in the hotel where he took a room after he had gotten his wealth. The landlady feels sure he intended to tell her where it was concealed, but he was shot before he gave her the information.''

"But. . .I don't understand. That has been years ago. Did you know before you went to California that the gold was there? Did you go with the purpose of searching for the gold?''

"No. In fact, Effie led Joseph to the discovery of it in a most unorthodox way. She fell, striking her head on the bedpost and at the same time dislodging a gold nugget. It rattled when the bedstead moved even slightly. Joseph was trying to stop the rattle so Effie could sleep when he discovered the poke of gold.''

"It's a wonder someone else hadn't already discovered it. It's been more than ten years. . .''

"Only two tenants, both elderly gentlemen, stayed in the room after Charles's death. I'm sure it never crossed their minds to go on an inch-by-inch treasure hunt. Anyway, I think God kept the gold hidden just for Effie.''

"And. . .how did you know it belonged to Charles?''

"It was in Charles's old room for one thing, but the conclusive evidence was a note Charles left in the bag instructing the landlady to see that Effie got the bag of wealth in the event anything happened to him. Effie has the note.''

"A-And I l-love the n-note better than the g-gold!'' Effie spoke up. "It l-lets me know that my f-father really cared for m-me!''

"I'm so glad for you, Effie!''

"Joseph and I got the scare of our lives on the train.''

"Afraid you'd be robbed?''

"No. Someone had stolen some gold, and the law officers searched everybody and everything before we left the Los Angeles station."

"What did they do when they discovered the cracker box filled with gold?"

"They didn't. Mrs. Bimski had thought to put crackers in the mouth of the box. The police supposed Joseph was taking the crackers for Effie's benefit."

"Effie, whatever will you do with all that money?" teased Charlotte.

"B-Build a church for M-Matthew in T-Texas and a s-school for A-Amy's children here in N-New M-Mexico."

"Why, you generous soul!"

"I h-had a d-dream. I m-must do th-this. T-Tell her about it, A-Amy. I think G-God wanted me to g-go to C-California to f-find the money."

"Effie didn't sleep well on the train en route to California. I thought she was overly excited, but she said every time she went to sleep she had a recurring dream. In the dream someone handed her a bag of gold, and a big white angel told her that she was to build Matthew a church in The Springs with part of the gold in the bag."

"A-And that s-someday there would be a g-great revival th-there."

"How very strange!"

"But b-besides f-finding the money, I v-visited F-Father's grave, too."

As the carriage swayed gently over the flat, sandy country, Effie's eyelids drooped and she curled up on the daybed. Charlotte spread an afghan over her, and she and J.J. slept peacefully the rest of the way to Caprock. Charlotte and Amy conversed in hushed tones so as not to disturb the sleepers.

"Was Effie injured when she hit her head on the bedstead?"

"Yes, she had a great bluish knot on her forehead for several days. The doctor ordered bed rest until it went down."

"She didn't suffer any aftereffects of the injury?"

"It doesn't seem so. The doctor called me aside and asked me to keep a close watch on her for the next few weeks. The danger is blood clots. One could develop suddenly and go to her brain or heart. He suggested I keep her quiet and fairly inactive. But however will I do that when she sees Pet? They'll be romping and roaming again with their magic bucket."

"Magic bucket?"

"Yes. Effie has taught Pet to carry a bucket with a rope handle between her teeth. And it's simply no telling what they'll bring home in that bucket! Once it was quail eggs—enough to make a pound cake. Sometimes it's pinon nuts. Sometimes berries. She even brought an injured bird once!"

"Now if that isn't quaint! Don't you know that horse has missed Effie!"

"Your mother and father have been taking care of the pony for her."

"At the stage stop?"

"Yes."

"I must see that magic bucket."

"You'll have to come to the ranch. We left the bucket there."

Effie opened her eyes when the carriage stopped at Caprock. "We're here, Effie," Amy said softly.

167

Grace heard the approach of the stage and sent Sandra for the animal. As Effie stepped off the coach, Sandra handed the lead rope to her.

"Sandra Grimes!" Amy cried joyfully. "Imagine seeing you here!" Amy swept her former student into her arms. "You look. . .wonderful. My, how you have changed!"

"But Miss Amy, you haven't changed one bit!"

Effie crooned to Pet, but her mind was not at peace. Martha had sent her to this desolate country to escape Claude Grimes. Now that Sandra (whom she remembered from school as an impudent tomboy called Sonny) had found them, Effie thought it likely that Claude would find her here also. Certainly, Sandra Grimes had changed from a swearing terror to a charming young lady, and Effie would not have recognized her had not Amy called her name. But her brother had not changed. He still stole, drank, and kidnapped. Memories flooded back, sending a shudder down Effie's spine.

"You'll come home with us, of course, Sandra?" insisted Amy.

"I'll be out there in a couple of days," promised Sandra. "Mrs. Browning and I are in the midst of a redecorating project here at the Inn. We're making new curtains and turning hems on the linens."

"Don't feel obligated to me, Sandra. . ." Grace began.

"I don't like to leave unfinished projects," Sandra returned. "This will give Amy time to get settled from her trip."

"But what's the hurry, Amy?" queried Grace. "You'll stay for dinner?"

"Thank you, Grace, but we've munched all the way,

and I'm eager to get back to my cottage. East or west, home is best, you know."

The sight of the cracker tin amused Grace as it had Charlotte. "Why, Joseph," she teased, "are you so hungry that you must carry crackers to sustain yourself?"

"These are Effie's," he said, keeping a remarkably straight face. "I brought them along just for her."

Charlotte and Amy exchanged glances of suppressed mirth.

"But next week, I plan to take these crackers with me when I go to the bank over in Texas." Joseph, still holding the controversial cracker box, gathered the luggage to go. Amy could almost feel the ache of his arm from the long hours of heavy weight.

"Dave will bring Pet along in the stock wagon," Grace said.

"Th-Thank you, Mrs. B-Browning, for k-keeping P-Pet."

"Pet was no trouble, Effie, but it's Sandra you need to thank. She took good care of your horse."

Effie lapsed into a moody silence on the way to the ranch. Worry that Claude Grimes would find her dug trenches in her soul.

"Cheer up, Effie!" encouraged Amy. "Dave will be along with Pet in a little while."

"I-I know."

"Don't you feel well, love?"

"I f-feel o-okay. . .o-outside, but I d-don't inside."

"What's bothering you?"

"There's n-no p-place to h-hide."

"The gold?"

"No-No. M-Me."

"Why should you want to hide, dear?"

"From C-Claude G-Grimes. Now that S-Sonny is h-here, he's s-sure to find m-me."

"You poor darling. I forgot to tell you. You don't have to worry about Claude Grimes ever again. Sandra told me that he is in prison way up in Kansas for many years."

"In p-prison?"

"Yes. He committed one crime too many, and the law caught up with him. Now let your mind rest."

Still Effie remained quiet, thinking. Nearing home, she spoke what was on her troubled mind. "J-Joseph?"

"Yes, Effie?"

"J-Just in *case* C-Claude Grimes gets l-loose and f-finds me. . .or a-anything else h-happens to me, will you be th-the administrator o-over the g-gold that F-Father left me?"

"Why, Effie, I'm sure Claude Grimes will not escape from prison or. . ."

"S-See that M-Matthew gets all he n-needs for his ch-church in The S-Springs. . .and s-see that a n-nice school is b-built here in th-the territory c-close enough for your own ch-children to a-attend s-someday. It w-would be so nice if S-Sonny could be the t-teacher. . ."

"Oh, wouldn't that be nice, Joseph?" Amy exclaimed. "I'd love to have Sandra near us!"

"And the r-rest w-would be y-yours for b-being so k-kind to m-me in my f-father's s-stead when I was a l-little child. I o-only wish Mrs. B-Bimski would have k-kept just o-one nugget for all the k-kindness she showed F-Father and for the h-headstone."

"Stop it, Effie," laughed Joseph. "You sound as if you're making out your last will and testament, and you're

170

destined to outlive me!"

"I-I know I'm b-being silly. But j-just in c-case, Joseph."

Chapter 21

Matthew's Dream

"*I* had the strangest dream, Pauline. I've never had a dream that seemed so. . .real." Matthew stretched his long legs and yawned.

"Was it a good dream or a bad dream?" Pauline splashed water from the ironstone washbowl onto her face.

"It was good."

"Then mayhap it'll come true."

"I'm afraid that would be impossible."

"Nothing is impossible."

"Then let's say highly improbable."

"Why? What was it about?"

"I dreamed that a big white angel with golden wings came to me with a bag of gold nuggets. The angel took some of the stones from the pouch, placed them in my hand and said, 'Go build a church in The Springs with these. You will see a mighty revival.' When I looked up to thank the white angel, it was Effie. Then the dream just ended abruptly."

"That's a strange dream."

"I was so happy I didn't want to wake up."

Matthew and Pauline divided their time between the Harris home and the Stevens parsonage, restlessly seeking their place in life. Matthew's unpopular preaching left him with no speaking engagements, and he assisted Henry on the farm or Pastor Stevens with church repairs to earn his keep. "God surely has a place for us somewhere," he assured Pauline, a statement of faith and not sight.

"He hasn't forgotten us, Matthew," replied Pauline.

They took supper at the Harris homestead that teemed with rambunctious younger children, a world removed from the sedate Stevens household, which had known only one gracious child in the person of Pauline. Matthew called their diverse families "the best of two worlds," but for the well-organized Pauline the rollicking bedlam of the Harris brood took some getting used to.

Everyone bubbled with exciting news, each bent on sharing his or her story of the day at Martha's supper table. The extreme difference between Pauline's background and Matthew's kept Pauline vacillating between the desire for many offspring and the wish for only one well-behaved child.

"We got two letters in th' post today," Martha shared after the blessing was said, the plates were filled, and the children quieted down long enough to eat.

"Mama! Have we ever, ever got two letters in a day afore?" asked Chester, astonished.

"No, not never, Chester. I 'bout had me a shoutin'

spell."

"Who was they from?" Henry asked.

"One was from Amy an' th' other was from Grace Brownin'."

Henry reached for the potatoes. "Writ at th' same time?"

"No, Amy's was writ first. 'Bout three days first. I don't know how come they got here on th' same mail coach. That's hard to figger."

"Pass th' biscuits, William," Henry requested, then said, "Mail is funny-like, Martha. Prob'bly they don't pick it up from Caprock but maybe onct a week."

"Likely."

"What cause did Grace Brownin' have writin' us? Matthew needs th' gravy, Dessie. She don't even know us, 'cept through Joseph an' Amy. What I'm meanin' is she ain't never seen ery one o' us. Is somethin' wrong?"

"She jest writ a short-like letter on perty station'ry. She said she wanted to rest my mother-mind."

"'Bout Effie?"

"Yep. She said Sandra Grimes was out in th' territory fer a visit to Amy. . ."

"Martha!" objected Henry. "That shore ain't no mind-restin' news a tall. If'n she's out there in New Mexico, that no-account brother o' hers is bound to learn o' Effie's where'bouts an'. . ."

"Henry, please lissen. You ain't lettin' me finish what I started. Yore jumpin' to all sorts of not necessary conclusions."

"All right. All right, Martha. But go on in a hurry."

"She said that Sandra asked her to write an' tell us'ns that her brother, Claude, has been sent off to a prison

175

in Kansas an' will be there fer many years to come with no chance o' gettin' released, so we don't have to worry no more 'bout his botherin' our Effie. She had jest learnt o' th' kidnappin' an' offered her sorrys to us. Poor girl can't help what her brother does. Miz Brownin' said Sandra was a good Christian girl now, one o' th' finest anywheres. Her grandpappy was a preacher, an' she made a school teacher out o' herself an' went to see Amy, but Amy wasn't back yet. . ."

"Back yet? What's she meanin' by that? Did Amy take 'erself off someplace?"

"That was explained in Amy's letter. I'm shore glad they got here t'gether so's I could understand what was goin' on out there, er else I'd'a been worried as to where Amy went."

"Well, where *did* Amy go, Martha?"

"Now that brings us'ns to Amy's letter writ afore Miz Brownin's. It was a longer letter, too, than Miz Brownin's, an' Effie sends her love to us all an' a great big howdy-do."

"Bless 'er. I hope she knows she's bein' mighty missed 'round here. Pour me some more milk from th' pitcher, Dessie. But you still ain't told me where Amy took 'erself. . ."

"Well, sir, all three o' 'em—Joseph an' Amy an' Effie—decided t'gether kinda sudden-like to take a trip out to Californey afore school started. . ."

"Californey?"

". . .and afore cold weather sets in. To visit Charles's grave."

" 'Tis a powerful long journey."

"Only two er three days by train from Lamy station,

176

Amy writ. Effie wanted to go real bad an' they jest somewhat felt it inside o' themselves that they should take 'er whiles she's out there with 'em an' that close."

"Close? It's hunderds o' miles."

"Anyways, that's what they set their heart on doin', Henry. So they was goin' to do it. An' I b'lieve Effie ought to get to do somethin' she wants to do on her grand-pappy's inheritance money. I'm right glad. . ."

"Oh, I'm gladsome, too, make no mistake," Henry confirmed. "She can tell me all 'bout my brother's burial place when she gets back here. It'll be 'most as good as gettin' to go myself. I'm awful sentimental 'bout my onliest brother. An' it'll make 'er feel better, with more fam'ly roots-like, to see th' place her own paw was laid away."

"Amy also writ some 'bout Effie's little cripple horse. It's white an' she named it Pet. Just Pet. Amy said she'd got it learnt to tote a bucket 'round in its mouth by th' rope handle. . ."

"You don't say! Ain't that clever?"

"A clever girl deserves a clever animal, Henry. God knowed that. They been goin' out ever'day an' bringin' all kinds o' things home in th' bucket. Vegetables an' nuts an' flowers. Even bird eggs onct for to make a cake. Amy an' Joseph 'spect they'll have to send th' animal home with Effie when she comes back to th' farm, she's gettin' so powerful attached to it. . ."

"Oh, goody!" Arthur piped. "When's she comin'?"

"Yeah, when is she comin' home, Mama?" Dessie asked. "She's been gone long enough."

"Too long," grumbled Alan.

"Amy didn't say when Effie would be comin' home,

but now that Claude Grimes is shut up an' Effie's out o' danger of his harmin' er kidnappin' 'er again, I'm gonna post Joseph a letter that we want 'er back as soon as possible."

"An' tell 'im we'll take keer o' that horse if'n he can get it here," Henry instructed.

"Please have 'em send 'er back in time fer school to commence, Mama," begged Dessie. "This is our last year in school, an' I want us to graduate t'gether. I'll be so proud o' her on commencement night, I'll be bustin'. Besides, I miss Effie's prayers turrible."

"Yes, post a letter," agreed Henry. "Post it so's they'll have it when they get back from Californey. Tell Effie we're all awaitin' eager-like fer her return an' to hurry home fast."

"How long did they plan to stay in California?" asked Pauline, the first words she had been able to thread in.

"No more'n two weeks, Amy writ."

"Let's think o' somethin' real special to fix up in 'er room an' surprise 'er," William suggested.

"That's a good idee, William," Henry acknowledged. "Like what do you have in mind?"

"Could we meybe get 'er a phonograph as a comin' home gift, Papa?"

"That's a mighty good idee, Will. She's a music lover. She been mighty unselfish to us'ns, an' we must try to do somethin' to show our gladness that's she's come back home."

"To *stay,*" added Dessie.

"Yes, to stay," dittoed Martha, reaching to the center of the table and moving the sugar bowl just a bit out of habit.

178

"Matthew dreamed a strange dream about Effie last night," Pauline smiled across the table into her husband's hazel eyes.

"Was it a good dream, Matthew?" Martha asked anxiously.

"It was. And it was so real, it didn't seem like a dream at all. I didn't want to wake up."

"Tell it. Dreams sometimes has meanin's."

"I dreamed that a big white angel with golden wings came with a bag of gold and gave me some, telling me to build a church in The Springs with it. When I turned to look at the angel, it was Effie."

"Sounds somethin' like Effie would do, don't it? She has a heart big as th' outdoors," Martha said fondly.

"An' Joseph used to call her an angel, remember Matthew?" Dessie reminded. "A bent-winged angel."

"Did you tell ever'thing in th' letters, Martha?" Henry questioned, wanting to miss nothing. He passed his plate for a helping of plum pudding.

"Amy said they was leavin' th' little horse with th' Brownin's. Joseph didn't want to be gone from th' ranch long, an' Effie didn't want to be gone from Pet long, so they was goin' to rush th' trip."

"So they should be home any time now?"

"They had ought to."

"I'm prayin' they had a safe journey."

"She said she'd post me a fresh letter when they got back from their trip, tellin' us 'bout it."

"It still strikes me strange they'd go all th' way to Californey jest to see a mound o' dirt."

"But Papa," Dessie explained. "That's th' way Effie is. Don't you 'member how she wanted to go to th'

179

territory th' first time when Joseph was drivin' th' stage jest to see 'er mother's grave?''

"I recall."

"An' 'tis somewhat comfortin' to behold even a grave plot, Henry," Martha added. "Think' bout our Robert an' how it heartens us to put a flower on.''

"When Effie gets real old an' ready to die, I think she'd like to be put by Rebecca," Dessie contemplated. "An' I don't blame 'er.''

"I wouldn't fault 'er fer that," Martha said slowly. "But in th' meantime, I'm mighty lonesome fer 'er to get back to Texas to my achin' arms an' give me one o' her beautiful crooked smiles. God never made an angel in heaven sweeter'n our Effie.''

"Ner more givin'," added Henry.

"Er more *fer*givin'," Martha said, with a sudden painful remembrance of the old unlovely Martha. Memory led her down a long road, then abandoned her to get back as best she could.

Chapter 22

Heart-to-Heart Talk

"*G*race sends her apologies. She forgot to give you your mail. She was so excited to have you back." Dave Browning handed the letter from Martha to Amy when he came to bring Pet home.

Amy read the letter and hurried to find Effie. "I have a letter from Martha, Effie."

"Is e-everything o-okay?"

"They're all fine. They send their love. But they want you to come home as soon as possible."

"H-How come?"

"They've just learned that Claude Grimes is in prison and no longer a threat."

"B-But I'm n-not ready to g-go home quite y-yet."

"Martha said Dessie wants you there for the school term so you two can graduate together."

The battle within Effie's bosom showed its raging effects in her dark eyes. "M-Must I g-go, A-Amy? I th-thought I'd g-get to s-stay all w-winter!"

"I'd love to keep you forever, but I can't be selfish."

"I'd l-love to s-stay here f-forever, too. B-But if M-Mother says I m-must come home, then I m-must go."

"I don't think she'd mind you staying a few more days until you get rested from your trip. School won't start for at least six weeks yet."

"I-I wanted y-you for my t-teacher, A-Amy."

"But graduating with your class will be nice."

"I g-guess, but I j-just don't know i-if I can p-part with P-Pet. I l-love Pet so much. P-Pet. . .u-understands."

Amy turned back to her work, feeling that her heart had gained many pounds of excess weight. She, too, had hoped that Effie might spend the winter and had eagerly anticipated the hours of study together in the snow-bound cabin.

Two days later, Grace Browning brought Sandra to the ranch, along with a single bed from one of the inn's rooms. Joseph assembled the bed in Effie's room.

Effie, realizing her days on the ranch were numbered, filled her hours selectively, giving Pet priority. Amy's warning for Effie to move slowly and to rest often seemed to fall on deaf ears.

"B-But I'm w-well, A-Amy," protested Effie.

"I know, dear, but the doctor said you must move about in moderation for several weeks."

The wilderness showed its first inkling toward autumn, and the evenings gathered a chill. Joseph collected cords of firewood against the impending winter, his favorite season of the year. Effie's nights were spent in the delightful company of Sandra, reading and having heart-to-heart talks.

"Y-You have ch-changed so much from w-when we w-were in school t-together," Effie said to Sandra one night. "Wh-What happened?"

"After my father was killed, my mother sent me to live with my grandparents in Oklahoma. Grandpa is a preacher. I found the Lord and was born again."

"Th-That's what h-happened to m-me!"

"I knew back then you were different."

"Y-Yes. I gave my heart to God in the w-woodshed when I was y-young. I r-read about it in the B-Bible."

"It's a wonderful feeling, isn't it?"

"G-great!" Effie pursued her favorite subject. "Wh-What k-kind of a ch-church does your g-grandpa have in O-Oklahoma?"

"He calls it a Holiness church. He believes. . .there's just one God instead of three."

"I d-do, too. And so d-does Matthew."

"Grandpa preaches from the Bible that Jesus was God come to earth in human flesh."

"E-Exactly."

"But most churches teach there are three persons in the Godhead."

"C-Couldn't be. Th-The Holy G-Ghost isn't a person."

"That's what Grandpa says."

"It wasn't a *person* that f-fell on the D-Day of P-Pentecost, or s-somebody m-might have g-got h-hurt." Sandra enjoyed Effie's straightforward, almost comical, reasoning. "And G-God isn't a p-person; He's a S-Spirit who is e-everywhere!"

"So that just leaves one person—Jesus. Jesus is the one God, who came in the flesh. As a man he was born the Son of God."

"Y-Yes. The H-Holy G-Ghost overshadowed Mary and c-caused the baby J-Jesus to be c-conceived miraculously, so th-the H-Holy Ghost has to be th-the same as th-the Father."

"I hadn't thought of that, Effie. You've studied that Bible, haven't you?"

"G-God showed me w-who He was. It was a g-great discovery for me. When I f-first got m-my m-mother's Bible, I s-studied the book of J-John every day."

"I like the Gospel of John."

"J-John knew who J-Jesus was."

"Yes, I believe he did."

"In the f-first verse of his b-book, he said the W-Word was God. Then he explained in the fourteenth v-verse that the W-Word became f-flesh and dwelt among us. Th-That was J-Jesus!"

"That's Grandpa's candystick Scripture."

"I l-like ch-chapter fourteen, too. P-Philip wanted to s-see the F-Father. Jesus s-said, 'He that h-hath seen m-me hath s-seen the F-Father.' "

"And Grandpa baptizes in the name of Jesus just like the original church did."

"M-Matthew does, t-too. I w-waited and had him baptize m-me before I c-came to the t-territory. Oh, S-Sandra, we are s-sisters in C-Christ!"

"Grandpa doesn't have a very big church because he preaches different from all the others."

"M-Matthew doesn't e-even have a p-place to p-preach, but he s-soon will."

"I'm sure he could go up and preach for Grandpa. Grandpa would love to meet someone else who has such a scriptural understanding of the one God."

"I had a d-dream that s-someone h-handed me a bag of g-gold and that I was s-supposed to g-give Matthew enough m-money to b-build a ch-church in The S-Springs. And th-that d-dream came t-true."

"You. . .someone gave you a bag of gold?"

"My f-father l-left it to m-me. I felt l-like it was m-meant for me to g-go to C-California. W-While we were there, J-Joseph and I d-discovered the gold F-Father had l-left for me h-hidden in the b-bedpost of the r-room he r-rented."

"Effie! That's the most amazing thing I've ever heard."

"Th-There will be a g-great r-revival in The S-Springs, and many people will accept this t-truth."

"Grandpa will weep for joy when I tell him. He thought he was the only one in the world who knew who Jesus was."

"So y-you see, I h-have to g-go back h-home s-soon and see that I c-carry out the a-angel's wishes. B-But I'd so l-love to s-stay here instead."

"You like it here?"

"Y-Yes."

"There's something special about this land."

"W-Would you like to l-live here?"

"Oh, I couldn't of course. I have my teaching cer-tificate, and I'll have to find a place to teach school. I can't forever be a burden to my grandparents. They've been awfully good to give me a home and provide for me. But they're getting up in years now."

"I h-have another p-plan, too. I p-plan to b-build a s-school here in the t-territory so that J-Joseph and

185

A-Amy's children will h-have a real s-school to a-attend. W-Would you c-consider being the t-teacher. . .s-some-day?"

"It's a brand new thought, but I would give it some consideration."

"You're so y-young and p-pretty, you'll p-probably get m-married."

The rays from the lamp caught in Sandra's golden hair. "I do hope to get married someday, of course, but so far I haven't had much luck," she laughed.

"Th-That's s-surprising."

"The ones I like don't like me, and the ones I don't like are the ones that like me. My best beau was in Grand-pa's church when I first went to live in Oklahoma. We were the same age, and he was a Christian. But he moved away before we were old enough to really get serious, and I heard that he got married recently. I want a good Christian man for a companion."

"Y-Yes."

"I've always admired strong Christian principles. Remember how I envied Pauline of Matthew when I was at Brazos Point, even though I was as wicked as sin?"

It was Effie's time to laugh. "Y-Yes!"

"I can just see myself now swaggering into class threatening to take Matthew away from Pauline. But even then I knew Matthew would stand for what he believed regardless of the consequences. It doesn't surprise me that God chose to reveal Himself to him."

"I w-wish J-Joseph and A-Amy had a ch-church here."

"Why do you suppose the angel named The Springs for Matthew's church instead of out here where there are no churches at all?"

"Th-There are more p-people in Th-The S-Springs."

"But the few people that are here need saving, too."

"J-Joseph and Amy will understand and t-tell them h-here someday. Y-You will help th-them."

"How do you know all these things, Effie?"

"I f-feel it h-here. . .inside me."

Sandra planned to stay only a week, but the week stretched into two. Joseph sent a wire to her grandparents imploring an extension.

"P-Please s-stay until I h-have to l-leave!" Effie wheedled. "J-Just a-another week?"

"I have to be home before school starts."

"M-Me, too. Amy w-wrote M-Mother that I'd be h-home in t-time to start to s-school with D-Dessie in S-September. Don't you w-wish we c-could stop the c-calendar?"

"Sometimes I do."

"Let's g-go h-home at the s-same time."

"Amy has already suggested that we ride the train together to Forth Worth, then I could take a coach north from there. That would save them making the trip with you."

"Oh, w-what f-fun!"

That final week, Grace rode out with a letter from Mrs. Bimski, excusing herself to return to the coach house after a brief visit. "We have guests," she explained.

Amy hurried to open the message. "Oh, Effie!" she cried joyfully. "Listen to this. Mrs. Bimski found a large nugget while cleaning up the room where you stayed. Joseph must have overlooked it. . ."

"Th-They all s-spilled."

"She's wondering how to get it to you."

"W-Write her by r-return post and t-tell her that s-she is to k-keep it in r-return for her k-kindness to my f-father and the lovely h-headstone."

"It must have been meant for her."

"Y-Yes. G-God always r-repays those who are k-kind."

Chapter 23

Golden Wings

"O-Oh, my h-head hurts."

The blinding headache started the night before the departure date. The suitcases were packed and sitting by the front door.

"I think it's the dread of leaving Pet that's causing Effie's headache," Amy told Joseph. "She spent the entire day today stalking through the woods with that pony and the bucket. I'm afraid she tired herself, too."

"I promised her I'd try to find a way to ship the horse to her," Joseph returned. "I'll check on the possibility tomorrow when we take her to the station."

Sandra solicitously sat beside Effie's bed, bringing cold compresses. The pain abated but returned with a sharp pang that made Effie cry out.

Far into the night, Sandra knelt by the bed of her spiritual sister, praying that God would touch the pain-wracked body. She sent Amy on to bed. "Effie will probably be all right by morning, and you'll need rest to go with us to the depot. Effie and I can sleep on the trip."

Amy left reluctantly. "Call me if you need me," she told Sandra. Then she kissed Effie tenderly. "Joseph will see that Pet gets to follow you home, love," she promised. "Try not to worry anymore." Effie tried to smile—a tired, crooked smile.

"Th-Thank y-you."

Sandra read from the Bible to Effie, rubbed her feet, and even sang snatches of hymns. Effie fell into a troubled sleep.

The grandfather clock struck the hour of four. "Sandra. . ." Effie's voice was thin and strained.

"Yes, little sister?"

"I'm. . .going. . .home." A hint of a smile quavered on her lips, barely visible in the faint light of the dimmed lamp.

"Yes, if you feel up to it," soothed Sandra, missing the connotation of Effie's weak utterance. And when the suffering body relaxed into a quiet position of rest, Sandra blew out the lamp and fell asleep as if drugged, thanking God that Effie had found relief from the ghastly headache at last.

It was well after daylight before Sandra roused and looked toward Effie's bed. Effie had not moved. "Do you feel better, little sister?" she asked quietly. "You needed that rest." When Effie made no answer, she got up to awaken her. "We have a long trip ahead of us today," she said, reaching out to touch the sleeping girl, who was covered with one of Amy's hand-pieced quilts.

Then she stopped, cold fear clutching at her throat.

Effie was dead.

"Miss Amy!" she screamed, reverting to Amy's schoolteacher title. "Oh, Miss Amy! Come quick!"

Amy surmised the truth. She put her arms about the sobbing Sandra, who condemned herself miserably. "I should have never gone to sleep, Miss Amy! Oh, can you ever forgive me?"

"You did all anyone could do, Sandra," comforted Amy. "I. . .the thing that I feared has come to pass."

"Had she. . .been sick. . .before?" Sandra cried brokenly.

"She struck her head a wicked blow on the brass bedpost while we were in California. The doctor put her to bed for several days out there and she seemed all right. But he warned me that complications could develop if she moved about too much too soon. Blood clots. I shouldn't have let her out with Pet yesterday, but she pleaded so. I could hardly refuse to let her enjoy her last day with the horse."

"I. . .understand."

"I really think she knew she was going to die, Sandra."

"Yes, she told me early this morning—about four o-clock—that she was going home. I thought she meant to Brazos Point."

"I'm sure she meant heaven."

"I think that's when she. . .went. She got real still. I thought she had fallen asleep."

"I'll see if I can find Joseph."

Pet nickered at the back door for Effie to come and play. "Effie's gone, Pet," Amy choked, trying to see through the screen of tears, hurrying to search for her husband.

Joseph saw her coming hastily across the prairie and knew something was wrong. "Oh, Joseph, she's gone!" Amy went limp in Joseph's arms.

A knife pierced Joseph's heart, but instead of making a clean cut, it drug across slowly with a jagged edge like a very old, rusted tool, prolonging the dread incision.

He remembered that Henry used to tell him to "bleed a wound good" so the healing would be without infection. His tears represented drops from his bleeding heart, as he lowered down his reserve and let them flow freely and drop onto Amy's dark hair. "She. . .knew her days were numbered, love. She tried to prepare us."

"You. . .think so, too?"

"I know so. Remember her asking me to take care of her financial affairs if anything happened to her?"

"Yes."

"That gave her away, but long before that I suspected she knew."

"When. . . ?"

"Back at Brazos Point."

"How did you know way back then?"

"She insisted on being baptized the Bible way before she left. . .because she really didn't think she'd ever get back. Remember?"

"I remember. . .now. Do you think Mom Harris suspected anything?"

"She wouldn't allow herself to believe it."

"Did we do wrong. . .by bringing her?"

"She would have wanted to die right here so she could be buried by Rebecca. It would have been her ultimate wish."

"But if we hadn't. . ."

"Now don't 'if' anymore, Amy. You couldn't change a thing if you wanted to. There are few things I would want to change. Her short life touched so many."

"You'll need to go tell Dave and Grace Browning. Dave can help you dig the grave right by Rebecca's. They'll want to help us lay her away. . ."

"I wish we could have bought a nice casket."

"I was just going to ask. . ."

"What, Amy?"

"Would it be proper to bury her in Grandmother Franklin's velvet-lined cedar chest? It has a lock."

"I don't know why not, Amy. It seems to me that would be perfect."

"And Joseph?"

"Yes, dear?"

"Could we have a little service for her even without a regular preacher?"

"That would seem proper."

"Just something simple. Sandra has a lovely voice. I've heard her singing about the place. Effie loved to hear her sing. She could sing a hymn. I have a hymnbook in the secretary. And you could read a passage of Scripture. . ."

"I'd be honored."

"Do you remember her favorite verse?"

"Quite well. It was in the fourteenth chapter of John. She loved the Book of John."

"The one about the mansions?"

"Yes. Rebecca had marked that passage of Scripture. Apparently it had been her favorite, too. Verses two and three. 'In my Father's house are many mansions: if it were

193

not so, I would have told you. I go to prepare a place for you. And if I go and prepare a place for you, I will come again and receive you unto myself; that where I am there ye may be also.' "

"Shall we. . .bury Rebecca's Bible with her?"

"Yes."

"Joseph. . .I'm glad we brought her here."

"I am, too." Joseph kissed Amy's trembling hand.

"What shall we do with Pet?"

"We'll take care of her for Effie, of course. The very best we can."

"That's not what I mean."

"What do you mean?"

"Pet will. . .try to follow us to the graveside. . .and she'll nicker for Effie all the way. I don't know if I can. . .stand it."

"Effie would want her there, Amy. We'll have to be brave for Effie. I wouldn't tie the horse up at home for the world. Effie and the horse had. . .an understanding."

"I'd best get back to Sandra, Joseph. She's taking it real hard."

Near the gnarled old mesquite tree, Dave and Joseph dug a grave next to Rebecca's—the spot that Effie had visited daily. Wilted flowers, just weeds in the eyes of the unperceptive, were scattered about as evidence of Effie's faithful visits.

Grace, Sandra and Amy bathed and dressed Effie in her best Sunday dress, a soft periwinkle blue one Charlotte had made with touches of lace at the neck and sleeves. Then they laid her gently in the softly lined chest with a clean white pillow beneath her head. A hint of a smile still lingered. Finally, they placed Rebecca's Bible

194

on her breast and closed the lid.

"You'll. . .stay with me a few days longer, won't you, Sandra?" Amy's voice carried a plea. "I. . .can't bear the loneliness."

"I'll stay as long as you need me, Miss Amy. I owe you a lot."

Joseph sat at the table in deep meditation, drinking the black coffee that Amy had set before him, not tasting even its bitter dregs. He asked for pen and paper. "May I. . .have the honor of writing Effie's epitaph?" he asked.

"No one else in the world was closer to Effie than you were, Joseph," Amy said. "And there was no one she loved better. No one could write a more fitting eulogy, I'm sure."

The pen scratched on the paper in sporadic stops and starts until Joseph looked up, satisfied. He handed the paper to Amy. It read:

Effie Rebecca Harris
Born: April 24, 1875
Died: August 10, 1891
Earth's bent wings
At last unfold
To heaven's perfect
Wings of Gold.
J.H.

Chapter 24

A Pet's Tribute

"*D*o you think Pet will return on her own, Joseph?"

"I think so, Amy. Let's leave her alone, and if she's not home by sundown, I'll bring a rope and lead her in."

A nebulous gray sky dropped a few tears on the backs of the mourners. Pet stood rooted near the fresh mound. Nothing had escaped her keen notice. The small procession turned to go, coaxing her to accompany them, but she refused to move, turning her eyes upon them reproachfully.

A hush filled the house, a hallowed sort of silence in which Grace Browning tiptoed about fixing a simple supper for the grieving family. Amy wept afresh at intervals, being comforted by Sandra, then vice versa.

"I'm. . .so glad I was here," Sandra said, "for the homegoing."

"And I'm glad you were, too. I don't believe I could

have borne it alone," Amy returned.

Grace offered to stay the night with Amy, but Amy objected. "You have your guests at the inn to care for, Grace. The Lord sent Sandra to be with me when I needed her the most. You go on back. She'll stay. . .a few days. Let Jim and Charlotte know."

Sandra nodded to Grace. "I'll be here for a few days yet." She unpacked a few necessities from her small trunk for the heart-mending hours ahead.

Amy listened for Pet's familiar nicker, but as evening crept into the sky, the pony still had not come home. "I think you'll have to go for Pet, Joseph. We shouldn't leave her there overnight."

Joseph took a rope and led the animal, still standing unmoved at the graveside, home.

"And Joseph, please don't shut her up in the stall," Amy implored. "Let her stay close to the house so she won't be so lonely."

But the next morning, Pet was gone, and Joseph found her back at Effie's grave. He once more led her homeward, putting her in the stall with plenty of feed.

"How's Pet today?" Amy asked on the second day.

"I can't get her to eat, love. She opened the stall gate with her teeth and went right back to the burial site."

"We'll probably have to tie her up with a rope for a few days, Joseph."

"I hate to tie her up."

"I know. But there's no other way to keep her here."

Joseph brought the colt back to the cottage again and tied her securely with a rope. "You have to stay, girl," he patted her, avoiding the injured look in her eyes.

"She knows Effie's gone, Joseph."

"Yes, she knows."

Amy willed her mind to look forward instead of backward. "Did Effie mention building a school in the territory to you, Sandra?" she asked while they were cleaning up the kitchen.

"Yes, she did. She asked if I'd consider teaching here. I told her I would give it some thought."

"Oh, Sandra, we'd love to have you!"

"The more I think about it, Miss Amy, the more I. . .don't know."

"If the government didn't pay you enough, Effie's money would."

"It's not money that concerns me. I'm not accustomed to much. I've lived in a barn before, remember?" Sandra stopped to chuckle. "It's the. . .isolation."

"We are a long way from a city."

"I. . .someday will want to meet a good Christian man. And who is there out here to meet?"

"That's something to think about. All the good-looking stage drivers are taken, I'm afraid."

"I guess I'll go back to Oklahoma if you don't need me. At least for the time being. If I can get to Oklahoma City by the first of September, I can apply to the State Board of Education for placement. They can put me where I'm needed—anywhere in the state. I'm not really particular. I don't feel any special. . .direction for my life yet."

"I'd keep you forever, Sandra. But I know you have a life to make for yourself. So I won't detain you. It's been lovely of you to stay this long. Let's see. . .this is the twenty-seventh. If Joseph and I could get you to the depot tomorrow, you'd have four days to reach your destination."

When Amy went to take Pet her water, a frazzled length of rope gave evidence of where she had been tied.

"Joseph," she said when he returned from his day of repairing fences, "Pet chewed the rope in two and is gone again. I don't know what we can do to keep her here."

"I don't either, love, but I'll go bring her back and try to think of some solution. There has to be a way."

After supper, Joseph trudged wearily back to the grave for Pet. The clouds lay in brilliant pastel layers that the sinking sun appeared to be tangled in. The portals of glory could hardly be more beautiful to the human eye than a New Mexico sunset. Amy and Sandra sat in the cool front room cherishing their evening together, remembering the past and talking of the future.

"Perhaps by the time you get Effie's school built here, I'll be ready for the challenge," Sandra weakened. "I have become attached to this wilderness."

"But even if you choose not to teach here in the territory, you must spend summers with us," Amy invited.

"Oh, I will!"

Joseph's heavy steps could be heard as he stamped his boots on the back mat. "Did you find Pet?" Amy called.

He entered the room, looking washed up. "Yes."

"At the grave?"

"Yes, with the handle of the bucket in her mouth."

"The bucket? Oh, yes! I set the bucket out behind the stoop this morning because of the memories it brought back. Since Pet was tied up, I didn't think she'd see it."

"She found it. Amy. . .was the bucket empty when you set it out back?"

"Yes, it was empty. Why?"

"It. . .has two fresh flowers in it now. Sunflowers. I have no idea how they got there."

"How strange. Did you bring Pet back?"

"No, I. . .couldn't."

"What are we going to do with her?"

"We. . .can't do anything more. She's. . .lying by Effie's grave. . .with the bucket in her mouth." The words tumbled out with difficulty.

"She's not. . .*dead?*"

"Yes, Amy." Joseph turned his head away to hide the stinging tears.

"I can't bear it, Joseph."

They sat in cheerless silence for some time. Then Joseph cleared his throat. "Amy, do you remember us reading in the Book of Revelation about the Lord coming back with a great heavenly host, all riding on white horses?"

"I. . .remember."

"Do you suppose God needed a special little white horse just especially for. . .a bent-winged angel to ride on?"

"I. . .oh, Joseph. . .I don't know, but. . .Effie would love it! The last thing I told her was that. . .you'd see that Pet followed her home."

"Pet would never have been happy here. . .after Effie left."

"You're right, Joseph."

"If there's a little white horse in heaven with bowed tendons. . .it'll be Effie's Pet."

Chapter 25

Joseph Missing

"*I*'ll be back before noon, Amy."

Amy opened her eyes when she felt the gentle kiss on her forehead. "Where are you going?" she asked.

"I'm going to get an early start on the chores."

"Wait. I'll fix you some breakfast."

"No, I don't want to take the time. I'll grab a biscuit on the way out."

"Joseph, the sun isn't even up yet! It's still dark."

"I know, love. Get another hour or two of sleep. You'll need it for the trip."

"Can't I help?"

"Just have everything ready to go when I get back."

A fall chill had stolen in from the north during the night, and Joseph's leather vest felt good. He hurried to the barn, and by the time he had filled the tub in the corner of the cow lot, the black of the predawn sky had bleached out to an early morning gray. He turned the young heifer in with her mother to save milking time. Every minute counted.

One of the cows was missing, so he hastily saddled a mustang he called Tumbleweed to search for her. Just so she was in the confines of the ranch's fencing was all that mattered. He could bring her back to the barn later.

He goaded the horse on, riding into the brushy north section, keeping his eyes roving for any movement. The sun slept longer these days, but it had finally decided to get up, stretching its arms of warmth across the western world.

Joseph thought he saw the lost cow and was urging Tumbleweed in the animal's direction when the horse stepped into a hole and stumbled, throwing Joseph from the saddle into a sapling. With the reins dangling, the frightened horse regained her footing and whirled back toward the barn, leaving Joseph stunned and afoot.

He tried to pull himself into an upright position but experienced a searing pain in his right leg. The walk back to the house was out of the question. He fell back to the ground, moaning.

Amy and Sandra had their breakfast and waited for Joseph's return so that they might start for the train station. Amy watched the grandfather clock nervously. "If Joseph doesn't hurry, you'll miss your train today, Sandra. I should have helped him with the chores. . ."

"Don't worry, Miss Amy. I can still make it by leaving tomorrow."

"I don't know what's keeping him so long. . .He's always time conscious. He said he'd hurry."

"He'll be in right away, I'm sure."

But the hours ticked away, and Joseph still did not come. Sandra watched the growing concern in Amy's eyes. By midmorning, her fears were perceptible, her concentration sketchy. "I just know something has happened to Joseph, Sandra," she worried aloud. "He's never been. . .this late."

"Shall I ride in to Caprock and get Mr. Browning?"

"I can go."

"No, you must stay in case Joseph comes in."

"Can you handle a mustang?"

"I haven't ridden much, but I can ride some. Do you have a gentle one?"

"Tumbleweed is our most well-behaved, but I'm sure Joseph rode her."

"I may need you to help me put the saddle on."

"Joseph will have the saddle. You'll have to go bareback."

"Miss Amy. . .I'll try."

"I hate for you to go alone. . .What if. . . ?"

"I'm not scared of outlaws or Indians or wildcats, Amy. Besides, the Lord will protect me." Sandra turned her eyes upon Amy bravely.

Amy walked with her to the barn. There she stopped in her tracks and paled. Tumbleweed stood at the corral gate, saddled and riderless.

"She's lost Joseph somewhere, Sandra. Take her and go—as quickly as possible."

The two hours of Sandra's absence were the two longest hours of Amy's life. She prayed and walked, fighting off obsessive thoughts of terrible possibilities that tore at her mind and burned her heart. What if something had happened to Joseph, who was her happiness? Her parents were gone, Effie had been dead eight days, and Sandra was leaving for Oklahoma. The only close relative she would have left in the world would be Jonathan, and she had not heard from him in months.

Amy paced to and fro in the yard, her steps growing hurried in her agitation. A prairie dog scolded, and a chaparral cock called, but she paid them no heed. Birds overhead winged south. The sun eased lower in the west, and she wished for a Joshua to make it stationary. Joseph had been gone for ten hours now, and she had no doubts that something was wrong. Badly wrong.

Dave and Grace hurriedly returned with Sandra. Dave's face was somber. "I'll find him, Amy," he promised, tight-lipped. "Try not to despair. I know you've been through a lot lately, but. . .keep your chin up." He whirled and rode off at a fast gallop.

"Did Sandra tell you about Pet, Grace?" Amy asked, trying to find a distraction for her own nagging thoughts.

"No."

"Joseph found her beside Effie's grave yesterday with the bucket in her mouth. She was. . .dead."

"She grieved herself to death. I was afraid of that. We had problems with her while you were gone to California, but Sandra suggested we find the bucket for her, and she rallied."

"The strangest thing happened. Joseph said there were two fresh sunflowers in the bucket."

"Sunflowers?"

"Yes."

"Who put them there?"

"We have no idea."

"Amy, Pet would have never been content without

Effie. They. . .belonged to each other."

"That's what Joseph said. And he said maybe God needed a special white horse just for Effie to ride when He comes back with His saints."

"That's in the Bible somewhere, isn't it?"

"In Revelation."

The clock struck five, every gong sending a javelin of panic through Amy's heart.

Chapter 26

A Neighbor's Reaction

"*I* heared somebody bought th' lot acrost yonder," Ruby said to her neighbor, chatting over the back-yard fence, her hoe resting against a knotted plank.

"It's a good passel o' property. Likely location fer any residence. Who was th' buyer, d'ya know?"

"They say a young upstart fresh married from out near Five Oaks bought it. Th' one what married th' per-ty daughter o' th' parson from Brazos Point."

"Well, I'm hopin' they make good neighbors. I declare, Th' Springs is growin' so fast, folks hardly knows their own next-door folks anymore."

"I don't think he's plannin' on building' no dwellin' there. . ."

"Land sakes, Ruby. What else would a body build?"

"There's other buildin's b'sides homesteads."

"They's businesses enough here fer a thrivin' city

209

'thout addin' more. What other kind o' business do we need, 'sides maybe an extry good cafe fer th' railroad hands?''

"Won't be no cafe fer shore. They're tellin' that it'll be a church buildin'.''

"A *church?*''

"You heared me right.''

"We shore got enough churches, Ruby, to convert ever'body in town. 'Cept my husband.''

"That's my opinion.''

"What kind o' church will it be?''

"Somethin' I never heared of. Myrt called it Holiness Pentecost.''

"Holiness what?''

"Pentecost.''

"Never knowed they was any sech church.''

"You know, like the Day of Pentecost in th' Bible.''

"Not th' Holy Rollers?''

"I dunno. What's Holy Rollers?''

"They're some religious group what run a revival over in Iredell. It's said around that they put somethin' on you when you go to their meetin's that makes you act strange.''

"Aw, Ruby, you don't b'lieve ever'thing you hear, do you?''

"No, but I got it perty straight from th' horse's mouth as they say. Them people b'lieve different from any o' th' churches we got in town. Myrt (she's th' organist from th' church at Brazos Point) said they done kicked th' young man outta their church fer pure heresy. She oughta know first-hand. If'n they don't want him out there, we shore don't want him here neither.''

"That kind o' church might bring down the value o' our property."

"That's what I was thinkin'. There ought to be a law again' churches comin' in an' messin' up a peaceful neighborhood, it bein' residential an' all. They're right noisy I heared. But I don't know of no regulations that would keep a body from buildin' any kind o' church they want. It's a free country, you know, with freedom o' religion. We might make it so miser'ble fer 'um, they'd not want to build here. . ."

"Now that wouldn't be Christian, Ruby. I think th' best thing fer us to do is not knock it till we know more 'bout it."

"I don't want to know more 'bout it."

"Well, I do."

Ruby went back to her turnip patch somewhat miffed.

Thus the controversy started, making Matthew's proposed church the talk of the town. With the good news from Joseph and with ample funds forthcoming, Matthew wasted no time in finding a prime lot in the booming little railroad town and drawing up his plans for a sanctuary.

The week that he ran his plumbline and staked off the building proved a trying one. The next morning he found his line and stakes all gone. Someone had gathered them up during the night and disposed of them. A second effort to mark off his foundation also met failure. The stakes were stomped into the ground, the work of an unknown antagonist. A canopy of discouragement hovered over Matthew like a dark cloud.

It was Pauline who came up with the solution. "Matthew," she chided gently with womanly sweetness. "Why don't you walk the perimeter of the land and pray over the place in the name of Jesus? Remember your dream? It came to pass. Now is anything too hard for God?''

After Matthew's prayer, the site was never disturbed again, and Matthew proceeded with his building program. In the midst of setting the posts for the foundation, the news came from the territory of Effie's passing.

"There's no need sending a wire, Joseph," Amy had reasoned sensibly. "They are too far away to get here for the burial anyhow. I'll just take time to write them a long letter giving them all the details we have. They'll want to know.''

Martha Harris found it hard to accept the grievous tidings and remained unconsolable for several days. A wreath was placed on the parlor door of the Harris home and on the church door.

"If'n we jest hadn't'a sent 'er away, Henry," she kept repeating. "Then she meybe wouldn't'a struck 'er head an' been injured. We should'a trusted God to keep her safe right here.''

"Martha, she could've been hurt here jest as easy," Henry reminded. "She was kind of accident prone, remember? We have to accept God's will.''

"An' anyway, she'd'a wanted to die in th' territory if'n it was her time to leave this earth so's she could be buried with Rebecca," Dessie volunteered. "It'd'a been her wish.''

But it was Matthew whom Effie's death had the most profound effect upon. It was he who suggested a memorial service for her.

"I've some confidences about my calling into the ministry that I've never told anyone," he admitted to Pauline during a time of reflection. "Effie is the reason

212

I'm a Christian."

"Effie? I didn't know that you and Effie were that close."

"We weren't. And my folks think your father influenced me to choose the ministry. But the truth is, as a very young man I never listened to your father's sermons. I can't tell you a thing he preached. I had, in fact, decided that living for God was not for me, and I was biding my time to take a different road in life. I planned to be a salty sailor and see the world."

"Why, Matthew, I never knew. . ."

"But it was Effie that convinced me that living for God was real. She lived like I thought a Christian should. When Mama was hateful to her, she prayed for her. I heard her praying in the woodshed. She returned good for evil, loving when she was hated. I began to watch her closely, trying to find a fatal flaw in her spirit, but I couldn't find one.

"You see, when I was about fifteen and ready to forget about religion, something happened to Effie in that woodshed. I knew that, whatever it was, her experience was genuine, and I hungered for that same experience. I know now that it was the gift of the Holy Ghost, for I later received it, too, but I couldn't identify it then.

"Somewhere in my later teen-age years, I decided I wanted to repay Effie for leading me to Christ. I said to myself, 'If Effie could, she'd witness to everyone she met. She'd be a great soulwinner. But she has a speech problem and can't. I don't. I'll take her place and spread the gospel for her!' That very moment I felt a special anointing upon my soul, and I knew that God confirmed my decision and would go with me.

213

"Then when I had the dream, and it came to pass, I knew beyond the shadow of a doubt that God had chosen me in Effie's stead, using her funds to open an effective door for me.

"I'll do my best, Pauline, not to be a disappointment to Effie. . .the angel with the golden wings. When we meet in heaven, I want to be able to tell her I did my best with the trust she left to me. One of my greatest earthly honors was to baptize her in the lovely name of Jesus before she went west."

Matthew's ministry took on a powerful depth, a dynamic dimension. He went to work with a determined will, convinced that the church, once completed, would fill with people.

A second letter came from the territory telling of the death of Effie's Pet. Martha, now able to read the letters herself, shared the details at the family table.

"Effie's li'l Pet laid itself down 'side 'er grave an' died," she said.

"Grieved, I 'spect," Henry offered.

"But th' undoin'est thing happened, Henry. Joseph found it with th' handle o' th' bucket in its mouth, an' in th' bucket was two fresh-picked sunflow'rs."

"It prob'ly passed through a sunflow'r patch gettin' to th' grave, an' a couple caught on th' handle."

"Prob'ly. Joseph had a real perty idee 'bout th' horse dyin'."

"What's that, Martha?"

"He said meybe God chose Pet to be one o' th' white horses in Revelation what th' saints er gonna ride on at th' world's end jest so Effie would have one her own size!"

"Now ain't that a beautiful thought? Joseph always

had sech nice-like notions. He ought to 'a been a poet."

"Oh, but Henry, he is a poet. A real 'un. 'Cause lissen here what he writ fer Effie's headstone: 'Earth's bent wings at last unfold to heaven's perfect wings of gold.' "

Henry pulled his coarse broadcloth handkerchief from his hip pocket to wipe away the river of tears. One of his children had made it home.

Chapter 27

The Yellow Telegram

*T*he stylish carriage came to a serene halt and the bejeweled beauty alighted loftily. She had no compunctions about leaving the driver in the last August heat for an indefinite time. Indeed, she was not given to thinking of anyone save herself.

She flitted to the door, giving the housekeeper who answered the clang of the knocker a condescending glare. "I've come to speak with Mr. Jonathan Browning," she stated haughtily. "My business is urgent."

Nina's small frame filled the passage way as if to block the vain girl's entry, but Marlena pushed her way past the maid into the sitting room. Marlena had no sense of propriety about entering the home of a single man. What Marlena wanted to do, she did, disregarding conventional rules or decorum.

In the early forenoon, the aged and wise Nina had

expressed her grave concern about the ruination of the master of the house, but he scoffed at her good-naturedly. "Nina, 'Lena may be rich and pampered to a fault, but she worships the ground I walk on. She'll make any changes necessary for my happiness. After we're married of course. She couldn't be expected to conform before we wed. It's just that we are from different backgrounds. I was reared by an old-fashioned set of rules while she is a modern aristocrat. I've been exposed to more righteous living than she. She'll soon adapt to my way of life. Don't worry."

But Nina did worry. "Can she turn hems and make bread and tend babies?" she pressed.

"We'll have a maid for all that." Jonathan threw back his handsome head and laughed.

Nina shook her sage head sadly. "Prosperity can desert a body. Think of all the Confederate currency that amounts to nothing since the war. Anything can happen. . .then you'll need a practical woman by your side."

"Now don't be a fatalist, Nina. I'd rather have someone that loves me than someone who specializes in turning hems!"

Jonathan, accustomed to the fretting of Nina, forgot her advice as soon as she had given it. She thought in terms of muslin practicality, he in terms of life's lace-edged thrills.

Marlena had kept Jonathan entangled in her shallow worldly pleasures all summer, setting such a pace that he had little time for deliberation. This, of course, was her intention. His early training was being broken down carefully inch by inch.

"Dahling, have you changed youah mind about going to that prehistoric place to visit youah sistah?'' she now asked, her great probing eyes holding him spellbound.

"I. . .haven't had time to give it any serious thought, dear. It's getting rather late in the year now. . ."

"That's exactly what Ah hoped you'd decide, dahling. Since you'ah not going to that dreadful country, we can announce ouah plans for a wedding. The society editah is crowding me foah some red hot news. You know how they follow mah activities breathlessly. They'ah just dying to get the latest scoop." She tossed her saucy head pretentiously, her jeweled earrings swinging like a pendulum.

Jonathan had grown accustomed to her showy jewels and gaudy bangles, once thorns in his flesh. She knew how, by her constant presence and then abrupt withdrawal, to make Jonathan miss her to the utmost—to feel that he couldn't live without her tinkling laughter. He lived the masquerade with her, never taking time to analyze her values or lack of them.

"I really am tired of being a bachelor," Jonathan conceded. "I've spent twenty-five years on myself. Set a date and we'll be wed."

"Dahling, Ah need at least three months newspapah coverage. It does take so dreadfully long to order mah trousseau, provide the attiah for mah bridesmaids, and plan for such a lavish occasion. It's a great social event, you undahstand. The greatest of the decade. Ah'll have to secuah mah musicians for the dance."

"Must we have a dance, Marlena?"

Marlena ignored the hint of reproach. "We simply *must*. It's expected in ouah social circle."

"But in honor of my deceased parents who didn't hold

219

with dancing. . ."

"Oh, foah the sake of the saints, Jonathan, you won't be requiahed to do but a few small dance steps with me and each of mah attendants." She gave him the irresistible pouting look that always swung the argument in her favor. "And then you can sit on the sidelines the rest of youah life!"

"You won't serve wine, will you, dear?" Memories of the last drunken party still stalked Jonathan.

"But Jonathan, dahling, it's customary. You don't have to pahtake, except foah the wedding toast. That won't ruin youah precious morals." Just a touch of scorn reached through to torture Jonathan.

"I'll just be glad when the social part is all over and we have each other. It's you I'm interested in and not the dances, drinking, and parties!" Jonathan mustered up a bit of vehemence in his tone.

"But the pahties make it all so glamorous!"

"Let's make it a Christmas wedding. Wouldn't that be cozy? Holly and mistletoe and. . ."

"But what about the weathah, dahling? The photographahs, and reportahs, and guests simply *can't* be snowed in. That would ruin the whole effect of the fabulous wedding!"

"That is something to think about."

"And remember, dahling, that Ah wish to go to New Yoahk for a honeymoon. Can't you imagine what a trip to New Yoahk would do for the *Gazette?*"

"I remember, love. Do I have any voice at all in the ceremony?"

"You'ah to choose the groomsmen, dahling. Certainly, you'll want Rudolph Gattsberg for the best man since he's ouah closest family friend and is very wealthy. . ."

"He wasn't a friend of the Browning family."

"But for the society page, Jonathan dahling, no one else would hold the eminence. Simply no one. No, it will *have* to be Rudolph."

"I. . .when does this engagement become official?"

"When you present me with the diamond, dahling. You'll make it a very lahge one, of coahse. I'll want a photographah for the presentation. In order for it to make the papah this weekend, you'll have only two days for the selection."

"I'd. . .like to invite Amy and Joseph to the wedding."

"I'll see if I can find room for them on my exhaustive list—though if I remember your puritan sistah correctly, she'll feel dreadfully out of place at the pahties."

"And about the house, Marlena. I'll have it redecorated. I hope that the furnishings that I have here will suffice. Many of them belonged to my parents and grandparents and are of sentimental value to me."

"I'm not much on silly sentiment, Jonathan, but if you insist. . .We will need to build servant's quartahs out back, howevah."

"Servant's quarters? I have Nina, and she already has her room. . ."

"I'll need at least two maids, Jonathan. Mumsy said I could bring Gladys, my nursemaid who does my hair and clothes. We'll need one more besides. . ."

Nina passed the door and picked this prime opportunity to state her position. "I won't be available to work for you, Miss," she said, all pretense peeled away, leaving bald frankness, as was Nina's way.

"I wouldn't want you anyhow, dahling," Marlena's

voice nipped the air with a chilling frost.

Jonathan started to object, but Marlena silenced him with a knowing look. "She'd cause nothing but trouble, treating you as if you were yet a five-yeah-old child, instead of the big, handsome adult that you ah." She wrinkled her little pug nose at him, making her painted eyes wide and appealing.

"If you're afraid of the weather in December, then it'll be November."

"You get the diamond, dahling, and I'll get the calendah down and find those editahs something to splash all ovah the society page. Now. . ."

The clang of the knocker sounded sharply.

"Whoever could that be?" Jonathan jumped.

"Probably a peddlah. The town has been full of them this summah. I wish they'd make a law against all solicitahs. Beggahs, that's all they are."

"Nina. . ." Jonathan called, "Please get the door. If it's a drummer, send him away."

"A drummah?" Marlena asked, ill-concealed interest showing in her coy manner as she leaned to catch a glimpse of the caller at the door.

"That's what Nina calls the traveling salesmen. It's the old-world name for them."

"Oh." Her interest dropped perceptibly. "But why?"

"They had to drum up business by their door-to-door sales and. . ."

"Yes, this is his address and he is in," Jonathan heard Nina say, and presently she handed him the yellow telegram.

He read it slowly, then read it again, tightening his lips until they were colorless.

222

"But whatevah is wrong, dahling?" Marlena chided. "Don't look so pokah-faced!"

"It's from my sister, Amy. Her husband. . .has broken his leg, and she needs me to come at once and help on the ranch for a few weeks until her husband is able to walk again. I. . .can hardly refuse her. Father would expect me to see to her welfare. She *is* my sister after all."

"But, dahling, our wedding plans. . ."

"You go ahead and start on them. I'm afraid they may have to wait for finalization until I return, though."

"You mean that you love youah sistah more than you love me, Jonathan Browning?" It was obvious that she intended for the words to sting.

"I mean nothing of the sort, love. I am simply telling you that duty demands that I. . ."

"But you *ah* putting your sistah's wishes above mine!"

"Then, love, I have only one solution. We'll get married quickly this week, and you can go along with me."

"What! To that forsaken, heathen land? Pray tell, what would I do theyah?"

"I'm afraid you'd have to help Amy with the cooking and laundry. . ."

"Me? Do servant's work? Have you taken leave of youah senses, dahling?"

"I have no other choice. . ."

"You just go on to youah baby sistah, Jonathan. Go and be her ranch hand. Call off our wedding for a mere charity mission." Her voice gained momentum. "Forget. . ."

"Oh, Marlena. Listen to me, love. I'm not calling off our marriage at all. I'll do my best to be back whenever you say. But, dear, I must go. Surely you see that I must.

Amy has never asked anything of me before. In memory of my dear mother and father, I must help my only sister in her time of difficulty.''

"You ah maddeningly pious, dahling," Marlena sweetened abruptly, putting on a different attitude as easy as if she were changing a garment. "But *certainly* you must go. Ah wouldn't think about foahfeiting my publicity with a common wedding. . .and I wish nothing to do with the uncivilized West. Ah hope you ah fed up with it before you'ah theyah a week! Ah'll go ahead with ouah plans, holding the editahs at bay foah a date. That will be most effective anyhow!"

"I'll. . .miss you, Marlena. . ."

Marlena was in no mood for sentiment. She took her leave—was she just the least bit offended?—giving no notice to the wilted driver, drenched with perspiration, who had waited two full hours in the broiling summer heat for the inconsiderate passenger.

"Take me to the newspapah office at once," she demanded.

Chapter 28

The Betrayal

"*I*'m not leaving you, Miss Amy."

"I do need help, Sandra. But I won't let you stay any longer without pay."

"I won't take pay, Miss Amy. I owe you an awful lot."

"You've already paid your debt twice over. And now I owe you! If you refuse to take wages comparable to what you could make teaching, I'll be obliged to send you home."

"But, Miss Amy. . ."

"Effie left more than enough money to pull us through this crisis."

Joseph stirred, moving the injured leg, and winced. "Do. . .you think. . .Jonathan will come, Amy?"

"I believe he will, Joseph."

"But suppose he's married and can't?"

"Jonathan would surely have sent me a wedding

notice, Joseph. I'm his only sister."

"I don't know what we'll do if he doesn't come. I couldn't ask Dave Browning to take care of my stock and his, too. He's in the process of remodeling the inn."

Jonathan did come, bringing his Browning humor that exactly filled the prescription Amy needed to heal the pain of her recent tragedies. Looking at him now, she felt she had quite forgotten how handsome his rugged features were beneath the shock of unruly brown hair. She assured herself that no one had a brother so loyal and unselfish— one who would come across the United States to stand beside a sister in her hour of need. Her heart swelled with sisterly pride as she gave him a generous hug.

"What happened, brother?" he quizzed, sitting on the edge of the bed Amy and Sandra had maneuvered into the sitting room for Joseph.

"Horse stumbled and threw me out of the saddle, Jonathan. I'd never make the rodeo."

"Feeling better?"

"Lots. Dave got a doctor out to set the leg properly. It was a clean break. He said I should be getting around pretty good in two or three months if I take care of myself."

"We'll take care of your self," laughed Jonathan. "That report sounds great. I need to be back home by November if you can spare me."

"By then, we'll be shipshape around here."

Amy introduced Jonathan to Sandra. "This is one of my former pupils, Jonathan. The one I used to write you about."

"The one you called. . . ?"

"Sonny!" Amy laughed.

"The holy terror?" Mischief danced in his eyes.

"Yours truly," laughed Sandra.

"Amy, why you ever called her that boy name, I can't see for the life of me." Sandra liked the way Jonathan's eyes crinkled at the edges when he laughed.

"Miss Amy!" Sandra exclaimed. "Your brother looks just like you. You'd pass for twins. It's. . .your eyes." The "Miss Amy" always came out when Sandra was excited.

Amy smiled. "That's what people said when we were kids at home."

"Of course Amy is *years* older than I am," teased Jonathan, and Amy shot him a mutinous look.

Sandra moved about her work, in her pretty gingham apron, with new zest. Amy caught her watching Jonathan when she thought no one would notice. She brushed her sunlight-colored hair into becoming fashions, and her blue eyes gleamed when Jonathan talked with her.

Amy felt, more than saw, it happening. Sandra was falling in love with Jonathan. She studied Jonathan carefully to determine if the feeling could be mutual, but Jonathan seemed unaffected by Sandra's beauty or charms. He complimented the special dishes she cooked, and at night they enjoyed board games together or conversed in animated tones, completely relaxed with each other.

Sandra spent a weekend with Grace Browning when Jonathan had been on the ranch about a month. Amy strongly suspected that Sandra planned the visit to get away from the emotional pressure of her growing affection for Jonathan. Her absence gave Amy the opportunity she awaited to talk to her brother.

"Surely you can see that Sandra's heart is in her eyes

for you, Jonathan. You'll never find a girl of higher principles. Sandra is a real Christian," she said, oblivious to
the fact that Jonathan planned to wed.

Jonathan lowered his eyes guiltily, then raised them
resolutely. "Amy, I've promised to marry a young lady
back in our home town. You may remember her. Her
name is Marlena Frost. Reuben Frost's daughter."

"I remember her. . .foggily. I'm sorry, Jonathan, I
didn't know. . ."

"Of course you didn't. I should have told you sooner.
The fault is mine. If. . .I wasn't already engaged to be
married, I would certainly be ensnared by Sandra's
charms. She is. . .unique. She has a simplicity, a natural
sweetness, unspoiled by pretense, that is truly rare.
Marlena is. . .not at all like Sandra. She wouldn't. . .fit
here at all, I'm afraid."

"Jonathan, are you very sure you are doing the right
thing?"

"Marlena loves me, Amy. She spends every day. . .
trying to keep me from being lonely."

"Does Nina approve of her?"

"What makes you ask that?"

"Nina is a good judge of character."

"Well, no, Nina isn't too happy with my choice of a
wife, but like 'Lena says, Nina wants to keep me a child
forever and I'm an adult now. It's just jealousy on Nina's
part, of course, and a bit of a personality conflict. 'Lena
has been reared in silk and satin. Nina will get over it
and accept her, I'm sure."

"I had hoped you'd come out here. . ."

"Marlena calls this part of the country prehistoric.
She is accustomed to luxuries and maids and city life.

She's. . .refined. A real lady."

"Has she a true set of values, Jonathan?"

"She values me, so I guess she must have," he joked.

"What about religion?"

"She doesn't attend church, but she said she would after we are married, if I insist. And I'll insist of course. I'll go back to Pastor Hollingsworth's where mother and father went."

"You haven't heard from her since you've been here, have you?"

"I didn't expect to. You'd just have to know Marlena to understand how busy she is with her social functions. She is popular and dabbles in a lot of civic affairs."

"When is your wedding?"

"Around Thanksgiving. Can you come?"

"I'm afraid Joseph won't be able to make the long trip so soon. Can you postpone it a few months? Until next spring perhaps?"

"Marlena wouldn't hear to it. She's announcing it in the newspapers."

"Jonathan?"

Jonathan sighed, apparently weary with the interrogation. "Yes, Sister?"

"Are you really in love?"

"Oh, for crying aloud, Amy, what is this? The fifth degree? Have I been court-martialed? I'm twenty-five, financially secure, and tired of living alone, that's what! What does love have to do with it?"

"Everything, that's what!"

The discussion reminded Amy of their childhood controversies where neither won nor lost. "Let's call it a draw," Jonathan would grin, and she waited for those words and the flashing smile now, sure that they would come naturally. And they did.

Sandra returned on Monday, and the weeks passed in a sequence of sunrises and sunsets. The cooling autumn only increased her adoration for Jonathan. Amy chose not to tell her of his impending marriage. She mentioned it only to Joseph.

"Joseph, I feel that Jonathan is making the mistake of a lifetime in the girl he has chosen to marry. I've talked with him, and he's got his mind set. What can I do to rescue him?"

"You can't."

"There's nothing I can do?"

"I didn't say that."

"You said I couldn't rescue him."

"But you can pray and God can. Have you forgotten Effie's philosophy?"

"Oh, Joseph, you darling! I. . .had forgotten. But I won't forget again."

"That's my girl."

"Will you join me? Effie used to say when two agree on anything in prayer, the devil doesn't have a fighting chance."

"Sure. I'll join you. But I can tell you something. . ."

"What?"

"I've been watching Jonathan. He loves Sandra Grimes and just doesn't know it yet."

"But if he goes ahead with this wedding, he'll never find it out."

"Yes, he'll find it out. Too late."

Joseph's leg healed splendidly without complications. By the end of October, he walked about without crutches or the nagging pain. The doctor recommended nothing further than caution.

Jonathan made hurried preparations to leave. Amy waited for a visible answer to her prayers but found none. Sandra lost some of her zeal, her chores becoming perfunctory, but she smiled up at Jonathan for the last goodbye. Only Amy caught the hint of wistfulness in his farewell. Or so she thought.

When Jonathan arrived in Kentucky after a frustrating trip of many layovers, Nina shoved the society page under his nose. Marlena's picture in all her pomp and vanity usurped the entire page. "So she announced the engagement before I got here, did she, Nina?" The query was more of a boast than a question.

"She announced the engagement the day you left, but she didn't reveal the name of her fiancé."

Jonathan laughed gleefully. "That's like Marlena to keep those editors guessing. It's a real game with her. And a very clever game, at that."

"I don't see anything clever about it."

"Well, I'm back and ready for the big event."

"I hope you're ready."

"Can you imagine me a married man, Nina? Married to the town's most popular lass!"

"I'd suggest you reserve your comments until you have read the article," Nina was almost curt.

"Amy can't come to our wedding, Nina," he remarked, offhandedly. "You're the closest to family I'll have there. . ."

"I won't be there, either."

Jonathan's mouth fell open, and Nina continued dryly. ". . .nor will you."

The shock of the news article gave Jonathan an awakening blow. Miss Marlena Frost announced her intentions to marry socialite Rudolph Gattsberg, and the society editors praised the match as the best of the century. A grand ball would follow, with a famous dance band leading the festivity. Names of affluent city leaders were dropped here and there throughout the news article.

The stark realization of Marlena's betrayal encompassed Jonathan by degrees, beginning with a wild panic in his eyes, then the sudden drop of his ruddy jaw, and finally the pitiful sag of his broad shoulders. Nina's sympathy, which lay just beneath the surface, awakened to its fullest potential. A hurt directed toward her prodigy brought her up fighting.

"Don't you dare fret, Jonathan Browning!" her eyes flashed fire. "She ain't good enough for you—and never was."

Jonathan's bushy head went down. The bubble of illusion burst, and he stood face to face with his forgotten soul. How had he strayed so far away?

He let the newspaper slide to the floor in a crumpled heap and fled to his room, repentant and remorseful. There he made his peace with God.

When he emerged hours later, the traces of worldly pride had dropped from his countenance, and Nina knew that something momentous had happened to Jonathan Browning. He was a changed man, inside and out.

"Listen, Nina," he said, his face aglow with inner strength, "I've got to get back to Amy's at once!"

"Is her husband still bad?"

"No. I just have to go. . .now."

"Jonathan, you can't run from what's happened. It

wouldn't be proper or fitting for the man that you are. You'd best sit back and face it—and go on with your life."

"I'm not. . .running from Marlena."

"Then why the rush to leave town?"

"I'm. . .there's someone in the territory I've got to talk to. I think. . .I'm just beginning to live, Nina."

Chapter 29

The Diary

Amy stood by helplessly as Sandra tried to piece the fragments of her broken heart back together after Jonathan's departure.

"Jonathan told you he was returning to Kentucky for. . .his wedding?"

"Yes, he told me the night before he left."

"I think he's making a grave mistake."

"I do, too."

"Did he tell you anything about the girl he plans to marry?"

"He told me she was. . .my age, and that she was a social butterfly that didn't know how to cook or sew like. . .I do. He said it in a teasing way but assured me it was the truth."

"I'm afraid it is. It's devastating when your only brother takes the wrong road in life."

"I know, Miss Amy. Mine did."

Sandra went to her room early. Nothing in the bed-chamber had changed, but even the furnishings seemed to be crying for something lost. Fully decorated, the room nonetheless seemed barren and empty.

Sandra lit the lamp on the bedside table in an effort to drive the gloomy shadows into the far corners and chain them there. Absent-mindedly, she picked up the diary she had kept faithfully all year and leafed through it. Her life marched before her in briefly penned snatches and sketch-es, bringing bittersweet memories. She read bits and pieces here and there, dwelling especially on the pages that mentioned Jonathan. Her heart lay exposed upon the white paper.

"September 3: Miss Amy's brother arrived this morn-ing. He is precisely what Miss Amy needs to patch up the torn places in her spirit. The man is the epitome of my dreams—kind, handsome, good-natured. Something awak-ened inside when I looked into his dark brown eyes. I never believed in love at first sight, but now I'm not so sure. My heart is spinning crazily. It is evident that he has had a good upbringing.

"September 5: I thought the fluttering in my stomach would surely stop, but it hasn't. I feel the color rising all the way to my ears when Jonathan speaks my name. It's easy to cook when I know that he'll be here for supper. Today he teased me, asking how I got the nickname 'Son-ny.' No one has ever asked me that question before, and I have never told anyone. 'When I was a baby, my father called me his Sunshine,' I told him, 'and my mother shortened it to Sunny. I liked it. But as I got older and changed from one school to another, everyone took it to

236

be S-o-n-n-y.' I didn't tell him that I swore and fought to live up to the boyish title. He has begun calling me The Sunshine Girl. I look forward to evenings when Jonathan is in. I'm a foolish dreamer.

"September 10: Jonathan has been here for a whole week. He is the easiest person to converse with that I have ever met. He's well learned and interesting. He's telling me all about his native state. It wouldn't matter what subject he wished to discuss, I'd be his avid audience.

"September 15: I think Miss Amy suspects my feeling for her brother. I try to hide it, oh, so hard! But how can one hide joyfulness? I laugh often, feel light and happy. If this is love, it's all I ask of life.

"September 25: I've taken time to evaluate all that has happened in the past twenty-two days. Jonathan is friendly, nothing more. He obviously does not feel for me what I feel for him. We play board games and enjoy the company of each other, but I must not deceive myself into believing that something romantic can or will develop.

"October 1: It's getting to me. I have made arrangements to spend the weekend with Grace Browning. She's having special guests, and I can help with the cooking. I hope to get my thoughts sorted and alphabetized. I'm letting myself in for a big hurt.

"October 6: Getting away didn't help at all. Actually, it made things worse. I missed Jonathan so dreadfully while I was at the inn that I cried every night. Obviously, he was glad to see me back in my apron, but only for the cookies I bake—not in the way I imagined. I, Sandra Grimes, have been a fool.

"October 15: Joseph is getting better. He limps about slowly and says it won't be long before he's back in the saddle again. Jonathan actually seems eager to leave. He looks at me without seeing me, smiles without heart. Something is wrong. A sense of futility is pursuing me. I'm staying just inches ahead of it.

"October 23: Jonathan proposes to go home next week if the doctor gives Joseph a favorable report. My spirit is laden with disappointment. I made this a matter of prayer, but no answer comes to comfort me. Can I ever truly forget Jonathan Browning? My heart tells me I can't. My mind tells me I must. What a paradox!

"October 28: I asked God to open the way for me to talk to Jonathan about his soul. And He did. Jonathan was serious and pensive tonight, and I asked him if he was a Christian. He said he had once had a relationship with God, but had strayed since the death of his parents (four years ago). I told him about being born again and referred him to Nicodemus. Then we got the Bible down and looked up all the verses of Scripture about receiving the Holy Ghost. Jonathan has an open heart.

"October 30: Jonathan left today. The goodbye was ironic. He told me during his final hours here that there was someone else in his life—a society girl whom he has promised to marry—and yet when it came time for him to go, there was real pain in his eyes. My heart is torn and broken. For myself, but mostly for Jonathan. I think I know how it would feel to be abandoned on a lonely island.

"November 2: I haven't told Miss Amy my plans, but there's no reason to stay at the ranch all winter. She and Joseph have their own life to live, and I must get on with the business of finding myself—and employment. Jonathan is gone from my life forever. Miss Amy is as grieved for him as I am for my wayward brother. I understand her deep sense of loss."

Sandra picked up her pen to make the log's current entry, staring through the window at the late lingering moon, which hung like a golden locket from a strand of silver stars. She paused between phrases, her heart pouring onto the pages of the diary, first liquid, then drying into inky words that left her desolate.

"November 5: Dave and Grace Browning are planning a last prewinter visit to Sante Fe before the icy weather sets in and shuts them away from their grandbaby. They have invited me to go along and meet their daughter, Charlotte, and her family. I think this is my opportunity to end my visit with Miss Amy. I can take the train from the Lamy Station near Santa Fe and be back to Oklahoma within a few short days. I'm posting Grandmother a letter to that effect."

Pages were added to the journal daily after Sandra's departure:

"November 7: Saying farewell to Amy and Joseph wasn't easy. Amy cried like I was a sister instead of a mere friend and former student. We've been through a lot together in these last three months. I promised to return to the ranch for a visit next summer. I put a flower (one that I had made from ribbon) on Effie's little grave before I left.

"November 9: I love Charlotte and Jim and J.J. They seem like family. I had planned to go directly to the train, but they begged me to stay and visit for a day or two. They have a school here in Santa Fe for the deaf—such an amazing academy!—and Charlotte wanted me to apply for work there, but they are well staffed. Being in Santa

Fe is like being in another world. Such majestic mountains! I am fascinated by Lilly, Charlotte's Indian housekeeper. I could sit and listen to her stories of Indian culture for hours! Dave and Grace went back to Caprock today. They can't leave the inn for long. I almost wanted to go back with them. Back to what?

"November 10: Today I will board the train for the Sooner State. Charlotte and Jim will take me to the Lamy Depot. Lilly will keep J. J. A norther has blown in, and it's growing quite cold out. I just must get ahead of the snow and ice. I prayed long into the night last night. I sense an impending something, but I can't identify it. A part of me wants to stay here, but that is not logical. Grandmother is expecting me home this week.

"2:00 P.M.: Here I sit at the Lamy Station, holding my ticket and awaiting the delinquent train. It is running behind schedule. I insisted that Charlotte and Jim go back to Santa Fe. The weather is turning bad, and I don't want them to be caught in a storm. I hear the whistle of the train. Goodbye, Land of Enchantment."

Chapter 30

Two Days Too Late

When Amy answered the desperate knock on the front door, she thought she was seeing a vision. Or having a nightmare. Jonathan's six-foot frame filled the entrance. Amy shrunk from his tired, sunken eyes, which suggested a lack of sleep. Had he married and discovered his mistake so soon? *Oh, God, please. . .*

She looked about to see if he was alone, and observed the portmanteau he clutched.

"Where is she?" he croaked hoarsely, not waiting for Amy to recover her composure and ask his business back in the territory. It had scarcely been a week since he left.

In Amy's confusion, she assumed he sought Marlena. "Did she come out here, Jonathan? Did you miss her en route?"

"Not Marlena!" Jonathan cried. "Where is *she?*"

"Who?" Amy asked stupidly.

"My Sunshine Girl."

"You mean Sandra Grimes?"

"Yes. I must see her. . .at once."

"She's gone."

The word gone pierced Jonathan's soul like a deadly dagger.

"Where? Where is she, Amy? I'll go to the ends of the earth to find her!"

"I don't know where she is, Jonathan. She left with Dave and Grace Browning two days ago."

"Which direction? Amarillo?"

"No. They went to Santa Fe. She was going to catch the train from there back to Oklahoma City to look for work."

"Two days ago?" Jonathan bowed his head. "I've got to find her, Amy. Will you help me. . .pray?"

Dare Amy believe what her ears were hearing? "What's wrong, Jonathan? Sandra said she'd write me by and by and let me know her whereabouts. . ."

"I can't wait until by-and-by! You don't understand, Amy." Amy had never seen her brother so distraught. "The only woman I could truly love is at this moment vanishing into the unknown."

"You mean. . .Sandra?"

"Yes!"

"You missed her by two days, Jonathan."

"Don't say it, Amy. It. . .hurts. You don't suppose the people in Santa Fe would know her destination?"

"I don't know."

Jonathan groaned. "This is the story of my life, Sister."

"But Jonathan, what happened? I thought you were

242

to be married. . ." With the answer to her prayer standing before her, Amy was skeptical.

"I never loved Marlena. I realize it now. She had the wool pulled over my eyes. She was a. . .fake. Someone prayed. . ." He looked at Amy. "I think I know who. And God spared me from making the fatal mistake. Marlena is marrying someone her type. . .with my blessing."

"And how can you be sure you love Sandra?"

"I. . .guess I loved her from the start. I've never felt what I feel at this moment. . .for any girl."

"Sandra really cared for you, Jonathan. She left with a broken heart. She didn't say a word, but I could tell."

"Could Joseph lend me a horse to ride, and tell me how to get to the place in Santa Fe?"

"I don't think you'll find her there, but if it'll make you feel better, then go!" Amy was willing to agree to anything that would remove the torment from Jonathan's eyes.

Like a madman, possessed and driven, Jonathan took his leave on Tumbleweed, Joseph's fastest and strongest mount. "Two days too late," Amy heard him mutter, almost incoherently. The protocol of goodbyes was forsaken as Jonathan goaded the horse westward.

Joseph looked up at the murky sky, red and lowering. "I think we're in for some bad weather," he predicted. "I hope Jonathan doesn't get stranded on the prairie. There's no protection from the driving cold on the open range."

"I should have insisted that he take your buffalo greatcoat, Joseph. Oh, what if he meets with a blizzard?"

"We'll have to pray that he doesn't, Amy."

Chapter 31

The Determined Chase

*W*hen Jonathan reached Cristo Haven, he ground-tied the horse, which heaved, with flared nostrils, lathered and exhausted. Jonathan rushed to the door of the adobe house.

Lilly met him with a fretful baby in her arms. "Is this the Jim Collins residence?" he asked urgently.

"Something wrong bad?" questioned the frightened Lilly, her black eyes fraught with alarm. "With me Charlotte and Meester Jim?"

"No, I'm looking for Miss Sandra Grimes." Jonathan's eyes were bloodshot from the whipping wind.

"She. . .gone," Lilly said, humping her round shoulders in a gesture of helplessness.

"Where?"

"She go. . .far away. For work."

"On the train?"

"Meester Jim. . .Charlotte. . .take her. . .train."

"When?"

"Only today."

"They left today?"

"Only today."

"How long ago?"

Lilly shrugged her fat shoulders again. "Maybe hour. Two."

"Thank you." Jonathan turned to leave.

"You better no go. The weather. See?" She pointed toward the mountains, then made a grand sweep with her brown arm, calling his attention to a mist that rolled over the Sangre de Cristo range, damp and oppressive. "You take sick. Is. . .emergency?"

"Yes."

"You no take horse." Lilly's Indian mind thought of horses as nearly sacred. "Horse too tired. See?"

"I'll take a cab out to the station then. May I leave my horse tied here until I return?"

"Yes. No push him more."

"Thank you, ma'am."

"Welcome."

The route to Lamy was a well-traveled one. The driver of the coach Jonathan hired protested that the train would be gone, but not wanting to lose the revenue, he obliged Jonathan. Each minute to Jonathan seemed an individual eternity.

About midway from Santa Fe to Lamy, Jonathan recognized Jim's red coach as the one Joseph once drove. It still bore the "Collins and Harris Transport" inscription on its side. The converted stage was going the opposite direction, returning to the city. That surely meant that the train was already gone. *Two hours too late!*

"How much farther, boss?" he asked the cabbie.

"Little less than four mile."

"So close and yet so far!"

"Sir?"

"Nothing."

"You meeting someone coming in?"

"Trying to stop someone going out."

"Impossible."

"Is the train ever delayed?"

"Now and then."

"Today has to be one of those now and thens."

"As you say, sir."

When the cab swung into the depot, Jonathan made a great, dangerous leap, ignoring the warnings of the driver and the icy tendrils that slapped at his face. The train puffed and growled while the conductor bellowed his final "all aboard." Jonathan pushed his way doggedly through the milling throng on hand for the train's departure. He squeezed through to the boarding platform, bringing upon himself churlish curses from the faceless hordes in his way.

As Jonathan gained the station, he caught a glimpse of her. Sandra tugged at her trunk as she drew near the ramp, a solitary figure soon to be swallowed by the crowd that hurried for the train.

"Wait!" he pleaded. "I must speak to Miss Sandra Grimes! Stop the train!" The wind caught the sound of his voice and flung it back into his face mockingly.

The porter turned, nonchalant. "Tickets please. Take your place at once, please." Sandra fumbled in her handbag for her ticket.

He had almost reached her when she hefted the suitcase up to the porter, who held out his hand to hoist her into the impatient car.

"Sandra!"

Sandra heard her name and turned about, puzzled. "Did. . .you call me, sir?"

Jonathan made an attempt to relieve the porter of the suitcase, but the uniformed man slid it onto the train. "I must talk to you quickly."

"Oh, but my train is leaving now, sir," Sandra hurried on, glancing only briefly at the stranger, a shudder running over her. A lone traveler and nervous, she found herself grateful for the protection of the waiting car.

The conductor hurried her on, blocking Jonathan from her view. The thoughtless train whistled for departure, smoke pouring from its stack.

Frantic, and risking his life, Jonathan swung onto the train as it pulled from the station. "Young man, you can't ride on this train illegally," the conductor scowled. "Have you a ticket?"

"I'll. . .pay, of course," Jonathan smiled disarmingly. "But I got here too late to purchase a ticket. And my trip can't wait. There's seating room, isn't there? I should have asked. . ."

The conductor thawed. "Yes, sir. I'll see that you get a ticket. I thought you were. . .following the girl passenger. Cushion car?"

"That one." Jonathan pointed to the railcar that Sandra had entered.

The train sounded a final toot of retreat, and the great iron wheels drummed out their clankety-clank against the steel rails with rapid staccato. But Jonathan paid no attention. He was on the same train with the girl he loved, and his destination was of no consequence now. *Let it sleet, let it snow, let the blizzard rage.*

Sandra found her place on the sparsely populated cushion car, glad that tourist season was over and that she could enjoy a time of reflection undisturbed. Her apprehension slowly drained away, and she closed her eyes.

"That man looked so much like Miss Amy's brother," she murmured, half-aloud. "But of course, it's because I have him on my mind. It couldn't have been Jonathan Browning. He's in Kentucky getting married. A case of mistaken identity. Evidently he thought he knew me. But he decided I was the wrong Sandra. . ."

Jonathan made his way into the nearby empty coach, recognizing the cascade of honey-blond hair. Sandra's head lay back, her eyelids shut like the bank teller's window at the end of a busy day, the long lashes still and becoming, her angelic face free of deceptive paints.

He had found her—his Sunshine Girl—and discovered that he was weak with relief.

Chapter 32

Sunshine At Last!

Jonathan fell into a seat numbly, hardly daring to believe his good fortune. He never took his worshipful gaze from the image of purity that sat nearby, unaware of his presence. The past few hours seemed but a melodrama, a sequel of fiction.

When Sandra opened her eyes, a startled cry escaped her lips. Jonathan moved quickly into the seat beside her.

"I'm. . .sorry, sir. You look so very much like. . .an acquaintance of mine."

"An acquaintance of yours?" he grinned, and at the sound of his voice, Sandra gave a bewildered gasp that further amused him.

"Yes, sir, I. . .but you couldn't be."

"Was this a *special* friend of yours?"

"A very dear friend, but. . ."

"My name is Jonathan Browning." The lines crinkled

251

at the corners of his eyes mischievously.

"Jonathan!" Sandra's ocean blue eyes grew round with real alarm. "Has. . .something happened. . .to Miss Amy or her husband?"

"Yes, something has happened. . .but not to them. Something has happened to Jonathan Browning."

"You're. . .married." She said it matter-of-factly, her voice trailing off to a thin thread.

Jonathan laughed, a relieved sort of laugh. "No, Sandra. I'm not married, thank the Lord. But I hope to be. . .real soon."

"Then. . .what are you doing in New Mexico?"

"I've come for my bride."

"I thought she was in. . .Kentucky."

"No, she's on this train. That is, if she'll consider me worthy of her hand in marriage."

Sandra looked about for the girl Jonathan was speaking of, her heart beating wildly. "Where. . .is she?" It came out in a soft whisper.

"I'm sitting right beside her." Jonathan chuckled at Sandra's obvious surprise, then grew serious. "Sandra, I love you and you only. I loved you all the time and just didn't recognize the symptoms."

"But. . .your fiancée?"

"It's over between Marlena and me. She found someone else. Will you marry me, Sandra? Please say yes." Genuine pleading underscored his proposal as he reached for her hand.

Sandra, who had dreamed this moment repeatedly in her mind, quickly withdrew her hand. "I. . .couldn't. You're not a Christian and. . .You see, I. . .you are simply reacting to a disappointment. It's never wise to make a hasty decision on the rebound. Marriage is forever."

"But dear, please understand. I never loved Marlena in the first place."

"Then why. . .would you consider marrying someone you didn't love?" Her gentle eyes searched his face for a clue.

"I wouldn't expect you to understand such an atrocity, Sandra. It's only done in society. I was caught up in the rat-race of worldly pleasures. Parties, social flings. I never stopped long enough to evaluate my true feelings. I had a false sense of. . .security and well-being. An ego trip. Love had nothing to do with it."

"How. . .tragic!"

"Yes, that's the right word. But someone prayed for me."

"At least two 'someones' prayed."

"I know," he smiled at her tenderly. "And God was merciful. He pulled me up short, saving me from a life of heartache. As I told you back at the ranch, I was reared by God-fearing parents in the way of righteousness, but I. . .went astray. Marlena wasn't a Christian. And I. . .faced myself, a sinner. I remembered the talk we had about being born again, and I prayed for that experience. And, oh, my dear. . .God filled me with His Spirit!"

Sandra's eyes filled with tears. "I'm so glad! But. . ."

"You still have reservations, don't you?" Jonathan felt he must know the reason for Sandra's uncertainty.

"Yes, but not about you. About me. I'm afraid if you knew about me—my past—you would feel differently."

"I'll never feel differently."

"I haven't. . .a pretty background. My father was a bootlegger, shot to death in a tavern. Mother died a sinner, and my only brother is in the penitentiary. The only golden apple on the family tree is Grandfather Grimes. He's a preacher, but not a very popular one. I'm not from the. . .stock you are. I'm not. . .society material."

Jonathan threw back his head and laughed. "I probably wouldn't love you if you were. I've had my fill of society girls. I love you just the way you are."

"I was a swaggering, swearing, rebellious tomboy before I was saved."

"Does the Lord hold that against you?"

"Not now."

"Neither do I."

"But I'm not worthy to be a. . .Browning. To be your wife, or Miss Amy's sister-in-law, would be too. . . wonderful."

"Sandra, that is for me to decide. I watched you for two months on the ranch. You carried my heart around in the pocket of your little gingham apron, and I didn't even know it was gone. You're. . .everything I want in a wife, now and forever. Can you. . .love me?"

"Oh, yes! I do love you already!" Sandra blushed prettily. "I started falling for you from the time you set foot in Miss Amy's door on September the third. . ."

"You remember the day!"

"I'll never forget it. I even. . .began to hope that you would. . .love me in return. Of course that was before I knew you were engaged to be married to someone else."

"The engagement was the mistake of my life, Sandra. Nina, my dear old nanny, tried to show me that I was on the wrong road in life, but I was. . .persuaded by outside influences that she was jealous and wanted to keep me a child. But Nina will love you. She loves honesty and

254

simplicity.''

The train snaked its way north and east, gaining altitude, creeping over the mountains like a centipede climbing laboriously over an obstacle.

"Where. . .are you going now, Jonathan?''

"I got on this train because you were on here. We. . .I need to get off at the next station and return to Santa Fe. I left Joseph's horse there!''

The comedy of Jonathan's chase, coupled with his gorgeous wind-blown hair, struck Sandra and she laughed—a bubbling, happy laugh that quickened the beat of Jonathan's heart. "Do you *have* to go back to Oklahoma. . .darling?'' he asked.

"I don't even *want* to go back to Oklahoma! I just. . .didn't have much choice. Until now.'' The merry little laugh that Jonathan found so pleasing broke into a wave of lovely ripples. "I felt God sent me to New Mexico. . .''

"And the devil tried to take you away,'' Jonathan grinned, the tension of the trip easing, his nerves untangling thread by thread. "Shall we. . .be married at Caprock?''

"There's no preacher. . .''

"Dave Browning is a Justice of the Peace and a distant cousin of ours. He married Charlotte and Jim.''

"I'll wire Grandmother so she won't worry.''

"It's yours to say where we'll be married, dear. Had you rather be married in Oklahoma by your grandfather?''

"No. . .I'd rather be married in the territory. . .where my beautiful memories are,'' Sandra said dreamily, her head on Jonathan's broad shoulder, her lips close to his ear.

The train rolled into a clearing between two mountains, and the sun's rays burst through the clouds in sheets of ethereal light, forming a pathway of golden beams that reached into the heavens.

"Look!" Jonathan gasped, pointing out the curtained window. "The sun gives her blessings to me and my Sunshine Girl." He pulled her close. "Now my life is. . . Sunny!"